FORTRESS • 104

FORTRESS MONASTERIES OF THE HIMALAYAS

Tibet, Ladakh, Nepal and Bhutan

PETER HARRISON ILLUSTRATED BY PETER DENNIS

Series editor Marcus Cowper

First published in 2011 by Osprey Publishing
Midland House, West Way, Botley, Oxford OX2 0PH, UK
44-02 23rd St, Suite 219, Long Island City, NY 11101, USA

E-mail: info@ospreypublishing.com

ISBN: 978 1 84908 396 6
E-book ISBN: 978 1 84908 397 3

Editorial by Ilios Publishing Ltd, Oxford, UK (www.iliospublishing.com)
Cartography: The Map Studio, Romsey, UK
Page layout by Ken Vail Graphic Design, Cambridge, UK (kvgd.com)
Index by Sandra Shotter
Originated by PDQ Digital Media Solutions, Suffolk, UK
Printed in China through Bookbuilders

11 12 13 14 15 10 9 8 7 6 5 4 3 2 1

A CIP catalogue record for this book is available from the British Library.

www.ospreypublishing.com

ACKNOWLEDGEMENTS

I would lie to thank Beryl Hartley who gave me the idea of recording the changes in the Himalayan monasteries, especially those in the dzongs of Bhutan.

Tashi and Sujay enabled me to visit parts of monasteries, in Bhutan and Ladakh respectively, not normally accessible and pointed out architectural details I would have missed. In addition Emma Martin showed me many unpublished photographs of the Younghusband expedition, some of which are reproduced in this book.

Finally I must thank my wife Diane who has been an enthusiastic and tremendously supportive travelling companion, especially in hair-raising situations.

DEDICATIONS

For Alexander, India, Yasmin, Tiana and Lennox.

EDITOR'S NOTE

Unless otherwise indicated all images are part of the author's collection.

ARTIST'S NOTE

Readers may care to note that the original paintings from which the colour plates in this book were prepared are available for private sale. All reproduction copyright whatsoever is retained by the Publishers. All enquiries should be addressed to:

Peter Dennis, Fieldhead, The Park, Mansfield, NOTTS, NG18 2AT, UK

The Publishers regret that they can enter into no correspondence upon this matter.

THE FORTRESS STUDY GROUP (FSG)

The object of the FSG is to advance the education of the public in the study of all aspects of fortifications and their armaments, especially works constructed to mount or resist artillery. The FSG holds an annual conference in September over a long weekend with visits and evening lectures, an annual tour abroad lasting about eight days, and an annual Members' Day.

The FSG journal FORT is published annually, and its newsletter Casemate is published three times a year. Membership is international. For further details, please contact:
secretary@fsgfort.com
Website: www.fsgfort.com

THE HISTORY OF FORTIFICATION STUDY CENTRE (HFSC)

The History of Fortification Study Centre (HFSC) is an international scientific research organization that aims to unite specialists in the history of military architecture from antiquity to the 20th century (including historians, art historians, archaeologists, architects and those with a military background). The centre has its own scientific council, which is made up of authoritative experts who have made an important contribution to the study of fortification.

The HFSC's activities involve organizing conferences, launching research expeditions to study monuments of defensive architecture, contributing to the preservation of such monuments, arranging lectures and special courses in the history of fortification and producing published works such as the refereed academic journal Questions of the History of Fortification, monographs and books on the history of fortification. It also holds a competition for the best publication of the year devoted to the history of fortification.

The headquarters of the HFSC is in Moscow, Russia, but the centre is active in the international arena and both scholars and amateurs from all countries are welcome to join. More detailed information about the HFSC and its activities can be found on the website: www.hfsc.3dn.ru

E-mail: ciif-info@yandex.ru

CONTENTS

FORTRESS MONASTERIES OF THE HIMALAYAS: TIBET, LADAKH, NEPAL AND BHUTAN

INTRODUCTION

The Himalayan mountain range separates the Indian subcontinent from the isolated, aloof and mystical country of Tibet where the inhospitable and arid Jang Tang, the Tibetan plateau, is known to its inhabitants as the 'roof of the world'. This region of Asia is sparsely populated, and probably always has been, a consequence of a harsh climate, inhospitable terrain and high altitude. Its people have embraced Buddhism and have developed a culture and architecture, instantly recognizable, that loosely binds them together whether they belong to the Kham people of western China or the Ladakhis of the western Himalayas. This is a huge area that embraces part of China, the Tibetan Autonomous Region, Northern India, Sikkim, Bhutan and parts of Nepal. Geography and a political wish to remain isolated from the western world have ensured that this 'Tibetan World' is little known even today.

This is a book about the fortress Buddhist monasteries that are ubiquitous throughout the region. Whilst there is a difference between monasteries that were fortified and those that were conceived from the outset to be both a combined fortress and monastery this distinction is blurred in most of the regions under discussion. Only in Bhutan can a clear definition be made; elsewhere the dating of monastic complexes is very imprecise. An attempt will be made, however, to understand why and how distinct architectural forms developed.

Researching the subject has been problematical; there is a great lack of written or illustrative material. Plans, for example, are almost non-existent (Tibetan artisans are steeped in tradition, learning their craft from experienced and skilled practitioners). In addition most of the monasteries that exist today date from the 16th century and have undergone periods of rebuilding, repair and restoration as a result of natural and man-made disasters. The annexation of Tibet by the Chinese in 1950 proved devastating for the monastic communities and their monasteries; almost all of its 3,000-plus monasteries were destroyed to varying degrees.

In the Himalayas the reduction in the number of monks has led to many monasteries falling into disrepair. This is especially true of Ladakh or 'Indian Tibet' whilst in Bhutan the Buddhist

The relationship between dzong and monastery at Tuwa is shown here. Both appear to be monumental fortifications and the monastery has additional fortifications in the form of a walled bailey with round corner towers. A similar arrangement is found at Hanle in Ladakh.

penchant for butter lamps has seen many fortress monasteries (here known as dzongs) destroyed by conflagration. Many have also been severely damaged by earthquakes. Although the majority have been rebuilt in the traditional manner many of the defensive features have been lost. Fortunately the drawings and watercolours of Samuel Davies done at the end of the 18th century during an expedition from India into Bhutan have survived. The volumes of photographs taken at the turn of the 20th century in Bhutan and Tibet, mainly by British administrator John Claude White amply illustrate these changes.

In the selection of illustrative examples two basic principles have been followed: that there are remains of substantial fortifications or that there is documentary or pictorial evidence that military architecture was incorporated into the monasteries. Many examples combine these two criteria.

In addition I feel that brief digressions are necessary. In Tibet the secular nobility ruled their estates from fortresses also, confusingly, known as dzongs. Here, however, there was only rarely incorporation of religious architecture; the dzong had a symbiotic relationship with a neighbouring monastery although the two were physically separate. This is, today, seen at Gyantse where the dzong had a geographical and spiritual relationship with the nearby fortified monastery of Pelkhor Chode. A description of the dzong is included as it is the sole surviving dzong in the whole of Tibet; all the rest are now little more than piles of rubble, many destroyed by the Chinese in the 1950s. In Ladakh there are substantial remains of a number of fortress-palaces that incorporate substantial Buddhist temples and accommodation for monks. Together with the fortified monasteries they formed a defensive network for the inhabitants of this part of the Indus Valley.

Finally the Potala Palace in Lhasa, a huge monastic fortress with its attendant fortified village, is described in some detail. It is one of the world's great buildings and has remained basically unaltered since it was completed in the 17th century, apart from the addition of residential quarters for the 13th Dalai Lama.

CHRONOLOGY

c. AD 640	Buddhism introduced into Tibet.
1207	Mongol influence starts when Tibet submits to Genghis Khan.
1430–70	Ladakh divided into two kingdoms with capitals at Leh and Shey in the east and Basgo and Temisgang in the west.
1525	Kashmir and India are invaded by Muslims from Afghanistan led by Babur, leading to the establishment of the Mughal Empire.
1610–45	King Sengge Namgyal rules Ladakh and founds many monasteries and builds the nine-storeyed 'lion palace' at Leh.
1616	Nagawang Namgyal, the Shabdrung, leaves the monastery of Ralung for Bhutan.
1629	Simtokha dzong, the first of the Shabdrung's dzongs, built.
1635–42	Monastic sectarian war breaks out between Shigatse and Lhasa in Tibet.
1639	Tibetans invade Bhutan and are defeated.
1643	A further Tibetan invasion, reinforced by Mongol forces is also defeated.
1642	Gushri Khan, the Mongol ruler intercedes on behalf of the Gelukpas of Lhasa and installs Nagawang Gyatso as the fifth Dalai Lama.
1651	The Shabdrung dies but his death is kept secret.
1656	The first of seven invasions from Tibet into Bhutan.

1676	Bhutan invades Sikkim, and again in 1694.
1683	Basgo, in Ladakh, besieged by a Tibeto-Mongol army for three years.
1705	The death of the Shabdrung is revealed.
1714	Tibetans invade Bhutan over monastic disputes and are defeated.
1730	The last Tibetan invasion into Bhutan sees the Bhutanese sue for peace. On the withdrawal of Tibetan forces the country dissolves into a civil war.
1767–74	Civil wars in Bhutan caused by rivalries between the ruling Penlops.
1783	Samuel Turner, an East India Company envoy, visits Bhutan and Tibet. He records his journey and is accompanied by Samuel Davis who paints many of the dzongs of Bhutan.
1788	Southern Tibet is invaded by a Gurkha army from Nepal. Shigatse sacked.
1834	A Dogra army under Wazir Zorawar Singh invades and occupies Ladakh.
1842	Tibet is invaded in the east by a Dogra army, which is repulsed.
1864	Anglo-Bhutanese war over the Duars, Bhutan's southern regions.
1865–85	Intermittent civil wars convulse Bhutan.
1897	A major earthquake in Bhutan severely damages most of its dzongs.
1903–04	Younghusband leads a British mission into Tibet and occupies Lhasa.
1913	The 13th Dalai Lama declares Tibetan independence after invading Chinese forces are expelled from Tibet.
1949	End of the Chinese Civil War with a Communist victory.
1950	Mao Tse Tung sends the People's Liberation Army into Tibet and the country becomes a National Autonomous Region of China the following year.
1959	Tibetan uprising put down by the Chinese and the 14th Dalai Lama flees to India. The area around Lo Manthang in Nepal becomes the base for Khampa guerrillas.
1967–77	During the Chinese Cultural Revolution thousands of Tibetan monasteries and all the dzongs bar Gyantse are destroyed in an attempt to wipe out Tibetan culture.

TIBETAN CULTURE AND ITS DISTINCTIVE ARCHITECTURE

The development of the Tibetan Cultural Region

Buddhism has been the driving force in Tibetan culture. The unique, magical, mystical and all-pervading nature of Tantric Tibetan Buddhism has permeated all aspects and levels of society since its introduction from India in the 7th century AD. Until the 20th century it was inextricably linked with the secular rule of this vast region. In addition it has fashioned the nature of this area's art and architecture, education and politics. Foreign influences, apart from that of the Mongols and the Chinese, have always been slight, with the Himalayas acting as a barrier to influences from India to the south. This being said Tibet itself has proved influential in the history of the other Himalayan mountain kingdoms.

Initially, high-ranking priests known as 'lamas' and the aristocratic former secular rulers of Tibet worked together during the reigns of the 'Nine Religious Kings' to extend Buddhist influence and control from its origins in central Tibet. By the 9th century AD the whole of Tibet had been unified and was ruled centrally from Lhasa. Huge stone and mud-brick fortresses, the dzongs, were built to coordinate the secular rule of the provinces. Monasteries became widespread and monastery and dzong worked in tandem. The primogeniture system of inheritance, wherein the eldest child

The Tibetan Cultural Region

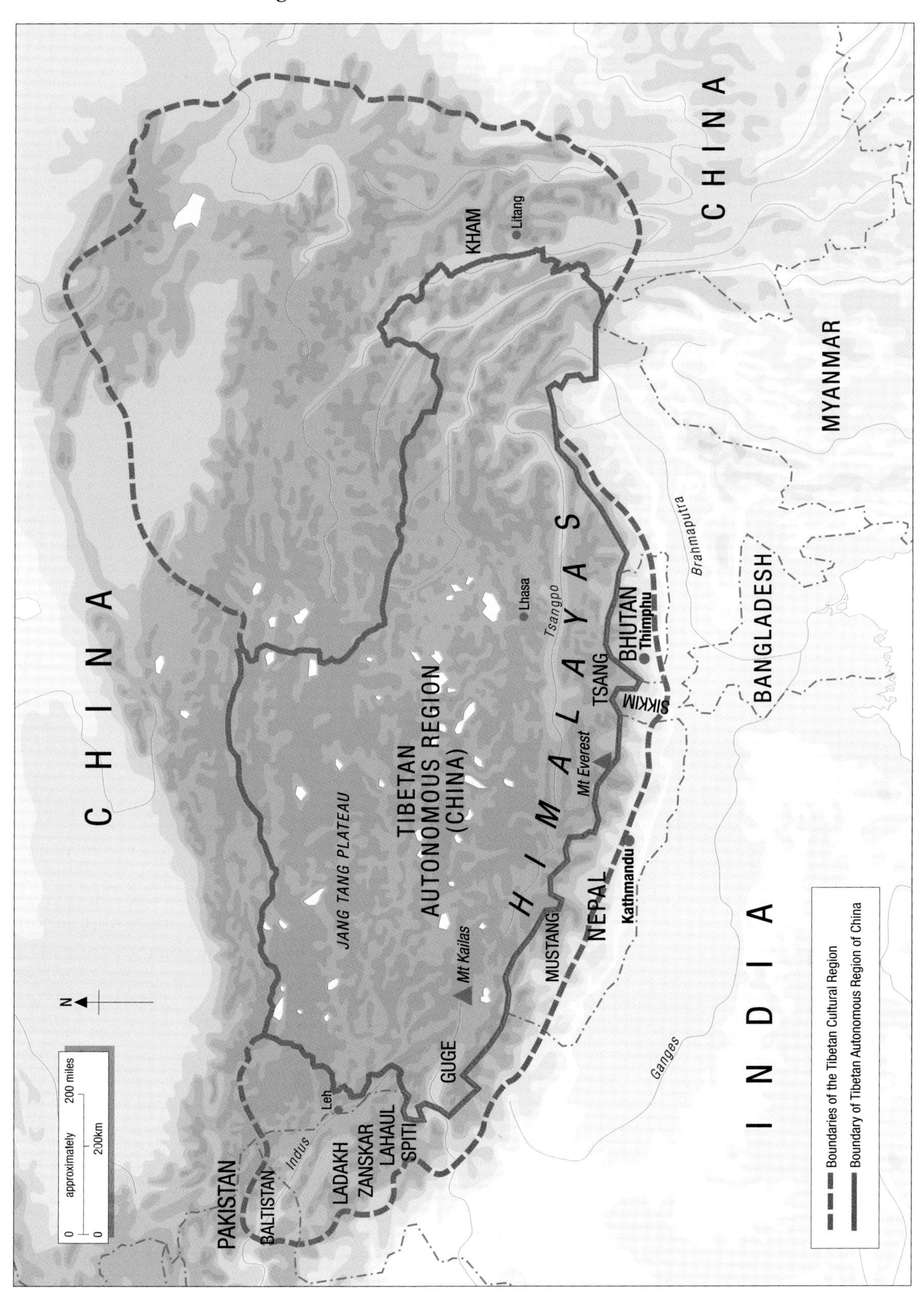

inherits, combined with a deeply held faith, ensured that there was a never-ending supply of recruits for the monasteries; at times as many as a third of all males were monks or novices. As a result monastic complexes came to dominate Tibetan architecture and over the centuries they continued to grow in size, wealth and power.

Although a unified Tibet was not to last, the establishment of a priestly caste with an equal status to that of the aristocracy remained. In the west the Kingdom of Guge was established while the Kingdom of Tsang grew up around Shigatse. In central Tibet a new religious sect came into being in the 15th century. The reforming Gelukpas, the 'Order of the Model of Virtue' – known colloquially as the 'Yellow Hats', became increasingly powerful with Mongol support and in the 17th century were strong enough to challenge the long-established 'Red Hat' sect of the Kagyupas who had the support of the King of Tsang. Gelukpa victory in the bitter conflict with the Kagyupas was far from certain until they sought help from Gushri Khan, the Mongol leader. The alliance ensured that the Yellow Hats became the dominant sect throughout Tibet by 1642 and Ngawang Lobsang Gyatso, a lama from Sera monastery near Lhasa was installed as the fifth Dalai Lama. The intention was that the Dalai Lama was to control all things spiritual with a regent appointed by Gushri Khan to oversee the secular administration. Such was the power and ability of the Dalai Lama, who became known as the 'Great Fifth', that he had assumed both roles by 1658, thus creating a theocratic state that lasted until 1950. Tibetans came to view him, and succeeding Dalai Lamas, as a god-king and under his reign monasticism and Buddhist culture flourished. The differing sects accepted Gelukpa supremacy and physical conflict between them came to an end.

Tibetan Buddhism spread throughout the Himalayas as a result of Tibetan migration. In the east the independent country of Bhutan was established; previously it had been an integral part of Tibet. Its creation was due to one man, Ngawang Namgyal who fled Tibet in 1616 to establish a dynastic theocracy, by unifying and carving out the country of Drukyul, the Land of the Thunder Dragon. In around 1640 he created the 'dual system' whereby he oversaw religious affairs and an elected ruler known as the 'Desi' handled political and governmental affairs. A code of laws was developed that underwrote the relationship between monk and layperson.

The Sikkim region was populated by the Lepchas until the 17th century when Tibetans from the eastern province of Kham migrated into the country. Within a short period of time the king and ruling class were Khampa.

Nepal did not achieve nationhood until the 18th century when the King of Gorkha unified the myriad petty states and tribes into a single Gurkha kingdom of Nepal over the course of two decades. Although a multi-ethnic nation had resulted, Tibetans had slowly penetrated the mountainous northern region.

In the western Himalayan range Tibetan Buddhism had been adopted in Ladakh and the valleys of Spiti, Lahaul and Zanskar, collectively known as 'Indian Tibet'. Although the Namgyal dynasty had ruled in an independent 'mild despotic way' from the late middle ages, the Great Fifth ensured that he was enshrined as the kingdom's religious leader, bringing Ladakh into his sphere of influence.

Whether theocracy or kingdom, however, Buddhist influence was all-encompassing throughout these regions and in many places remains so to this day.

A brief outline of a distinctive architecture

Building materials and methods

A corner of Ganden monastery near Lhasa, showing typical Tibetan architecture with its sloping walls, increasing window sizes and flat roofs. Behind is the huge wall on which painted scrolls (the Tanka) are hung during Buddhist festivals.

Both vernacular and religious buildings were built using the same materials and methods of construction. Techniques have remained unchanged for centuries until recent times and, coupled with the continuing process of 'construction, demolition and re-erection' of buildings, makes dating impossible and the region has not been the focus of attention for archaeologists. The siting of buildings was important, and in the case of fortified buildings, temples and monasteries, cosmology, magic and superstition played a role as important as the more pragmatic considerations such as a water supply and strategic positioning. The nature, form and building were supervised by master builders and architects, usually senior lamas. There were no drawn plans – scale and form are traditional and have stood the test of time. Buddhists reject the notion of permanence. The absolute belief in the cycle of birth, death and rebirth also relates to its architecture, with particular relevance when it comes to monasteries and temples. This has enabled Tibetan monks to repair, refurbish and rebuild these places of power in the traditional manner over the centuries, continuing to this day.

Labour was obtained under the corvée system whereby the vassals of the feudal lord or monastic lama worked for free as a form of labour tax – though usually at a time when agricultural demands were not paramount. Skilled artisans, such as wood carvers and painters, were professional and paid.

Unless built on a rocky surface foundations were substantial. The lower courses of all buildings were well built consisting of neat courses of rough-hewn field stone embedded in a mud and chaff mortar. Upper storeys were frequently made of mud-bricks, sun dried on their sides to prevent cracking. If wood was not available locally window frames, door frames, lintels, joists and planks were prefabricated and transported from wooden regions. Usually pine and oak were the timbers of choice. All wooded structures were constructed without the use of nails and the arch was never used, being replaced by beams. Wooden structures were usually replaced after 25 years, the average lifetime of untreated wood. Roofs were traditionally flat to preserve heat, covered with shingles (either slate or wooden), held down by stones and carried on wooden pillars.

The Tibetan architectural template

When built on flat ground most buildings are square or rectangular. When built on mountaintops or crests the contours are usually followed, particularly when defence is a consideration. Walls invariably slant inwards, usually at an angle of approximately ten degrees. This is a precaution against earthquake damage. In the lower storeys of buildings windows are absent or very narrow. As the building rises windows become progressively larger and those of the uppermost storeys are provided with wooden balconies. Windows are surrounded by wooden frames painted black, narrowing towards the top; these are closed by wooden shutters.

Internally the ground floor is levelled using pounded earth overlaid with stone slabs or wooden planks. Internally, the assembly rooms, halls, temples and passages are timber framed with mud-brick and mortar infilling. Intricate wood carvings are especially noticeable in monasteries and much of the carpentry and walls is vividly painted. Walls are usually coated in the finest clay and given a lime wash externally as a protection against the winds and snow of winter. This whiteness, however, provides an agreeable contrast to the black outlines of the windows and the harshness of much of the landscape.

Entrance doors are usually large and heavy, often iron plated and reached by a flight of steps or a huge ladder carved out of a solitary tree trunk. Entrances and windows more commonly face south to receive as much of the available sunshine as possible.

THE CAUSES AND NATURE OF WARFARE IN THE TIBETAN CULTURAL REGION

Religious conflicts, civil wars and invasions

Despite the perceived peaceful, non-violent, tolerant and compassionate nature of Buddhism the region has been almost constantly involved in internal conflict and subjected to invasions from without for centuries.

Superficially unified by religion, endemic conflicts between the various sects occurred throughout the 13th century and again in the 17th before finally culminating in a civil war, ultimately leading to the rule of the fifth Dalai Lama. This was followed by a period of civil strife and conflict as he attempted to reunite all of Tibet.

In 17th-century Bhutan the Drukpa Kagyupa subsect predominated, especially after the arrival of the renegade lama Namgyal Ngawang. This new threat posed a great challenge to the central authority in Lhasa who unsuccessfully invaded the country on a number of occasions in the 17th century.

This 19th-century miniature depicts a typical warrior of the steppes and plateaux. Armour and equipment varied little from the 17th to 20th centuries. The only change was the addition of the matchlock gun.

Bhutan was to undergo recurrent periods of instability and conflict owing to squabbles between the regional governors, or *penlops*, who ruled the country from the unique system of provincial fortress monasteries – the dzongs. Jockeying for power continued up until the 19th century.

Sikkim, known as Den-Jong (the 'hidden rice valley') to its inhabitants and Tibetan overlords, is sandwiched between Bhutan and Nepal. It was invaded by the Bhutanese in the 18th century and only Tibetan intervention liberated the country. The following century saw civil war break out between the native Lepchas and the descendants of the Khampa immigrants in 1826; it was to last eight years.

Nepal felt strong enough to invade Tibet between 1788 and 1791. Only help from the Chinese, who sent an army, rescued the country from occupation. In the middle of the 19th century war between the two countries broke out once again.

Ladakh, together with part of western Tibet, had been part of the medieval Kingdom of Guge and acted as the western bastion of Buddhism against increasing

Muslim belligerence. It was invaded in 1531 by the army of the Khan of Kashgar as a prelude to his ambitious plan to invade Tibet and plunder its rich monasteries. Paradoxically, when Tibet invaded Ladakh towards the end of the 18th century the Ladakhi king sought Muslim help in defending his country. Ladakh continued to suffer. Desultory raids by Muslim forces in the early part of the 19th century were followed by a Sikh invasion in 1834. This was designed to act as a springboard for a three-pronged attack on western Tibet that ultimately failed.

Fearful of perceived Russian designs on Tibet, which would potentially pose a threat to British India, a British diplomatic mission entered Sikkim in 1903 led by Colonel Francis Younghusband. Diplomacy failed and the mission turned into a military invasion and Lhasa was occupied in 1904.

Finally in 1950 after China had annexed parts of Kham in eastern Tibet the People's Liberation Army invaded Tibet. The weak and poorly equipped local forces were no match for the 40,000 Chinese veterans who had just defeated the Nationalists in the Chinese Civil War. This was to result in a period of death and destruction unprecedented in Tibetan history.

The raising of standing forces and militias

Although the population of the Tibetan Cultural Region has been estimated at between two and three and a half million people it was widely scattered and the region was sparsely populated. Only in the comparatively fertile river valleys, notably those of the Tsangpo (Brahmaputra) in Tibet and the Indus in Ladakh, were there significant pockets of population composed mainly of herdsmen, farmers and traders. Elsewhere large areas of the inhospitable Himalayas and the Tibetan plateau were inhabited by nomads, many of whom, living in tribes or autonomous groups were both physically and politically remote from central governments; they were, in the main, left to their own devices. This was particularly the case in eastern Tibet where the Khampa – fierce, unruly and dreaded warriors – lived in upwards of 20 disparate groups, which were ruled by petty kings, warlords, and monastic senior lamas until the end of the 19th century. Additionally, vast numbers of monks ensured that the male population from which an army or militia could be recruited was reduced. Some monks did, however, take up arms during the numerous conflicts that erupted throughout in the region.

Only in Tibet and possibly Bhutan were there bodies of professional soldiers, and then only in comparatively small numbers. In Tibet the numbers of professional soldiers in its standing army fluctuated greatly. In the 18th century, there were perhaps 20,000 men under arms, both cavalry and infantry, although in the main they were a citizen army rather than professional soldiers. This had dropped to approximately 3,000 by the early part of the 19th. Professional soldiers served for three years and then became members of a territorial militia.

In Tibetan monasteries many monks had specific and specialized roles ranging from agricultural labouring to medicine. One such group, known as the Dob Dobs, had the role of monastic policemen, which was necessary in communities that could number as many as 3,000. Trained in martial arts they were armed with a long knife and escorted senior lamas on their travels. They were both feared and admired for their athleticism. Monks such as these were certainly involved, both physically and politically, in the sectarian warfare and violence that plagued Tibet. It was noted that when the British fought the Tibetans at Gyantse in 1904 many of the most resolute fighters were monks and many monks left their monasteries and took up arms against the Chinese PLA and the 'Red Guards' in the 1950s and 60s

In Bhutan the power-seeking and warring *penlops* employed small numbers of professional soldiers to guard them and defend their seats of power, the fortress-monastery dzongs.

Elsewhere in the region the ruling elites relied on raising peasant militias when danger threatened. This was particularly so in Ladakh where each family was required to put into the field one man, armed and equipped for military service. At times of greatest threat every able male was pressed into the defending forces.

Equipment of the armed forces and militias

Throughout the whole region, each fighting man had, when fully equipped, the same basic arms and armour, which barely changed from the 17th century when firearms, in the form of the matchlock, were introduced from China and Central Asia, although it was not to become widespread in Tibet until the 19th century. This smoothbore musket remained in use until the early part of the 20th century and became ubiquitous. In Tibet the men were provided with 'A'-shaped folding prong-rests attached to the distal end of the barrel; their purpose was to provide stability when the musket was aimed.

In Ladakh, by the 18th century the head of each household had been provided by the ruling elite with a matchlock and its accoutrements. Maintenance was mandatory; in addition it was forbidden to lend, sell or buy matchlocks. Also available were arms and armour that were a legacy from the Middle Ages. Each man, whether professional or levy was armed with a sword, knife, bamboo composite bow, a quiver of arrows and frequently a spear. The use of slings was also common and the ratio of bows and arrows to matchlocks was approximately three to one. Cane shields and helmets provided personal protection, although the officer class usually had bossed hide shields of a north Indian pattern and metal helmets. Armour was frequently encountered and was composed of leather or metal lamellar corsets or chain mail. In Tibet the 'set of four mirrors' was frequently placed over chain mail. Composed of four, highly polished metal roundels, held together by leather straps, this provided additional physical protection to the chest, sides and back. Equally it was designed to reflect and ward off damaging spiritual assailants.

Artillery in the form of cannon was extremely rare; a few pieces had been obtained by the Tibetans from China and were used in the defence of Gyantse dzong in 1904. A variant of the Chinese catapult for hurling stones, similar to the trebuchet, was, however, far more common and was in use until the 20th century; they were found in the dzongs of both Tibet and Bhutan. More common were jingalls, the smoothbore wall pieces and swivel guns of varying bores common throughout India and China. Of differing sizes their missiles could be discharged over considerable distances. The larger-bored jingalls required three men to operate them – one to aim and fire and two to hold the prongs to reduce recoil. Like the matchlock, however, they lacked accuracy. Ammunition was usually lead- or copper-covered stones.

Tibetan passes are very narrow with steep sides. Defensive walls were quickly erected but usually not much higher than 2m (7ft). Those encountered by the Younghusband expedition were either abandoned or circumvented by his agile Gurhka soldiers. The walls here, at Yatung on the Sikkim border, were soundly constructed and appear to have loopholed crenellations.

Training and the method of warfare

Uniforms and regimental discipline were of little consequence apart from the elite troops of the Dalai Lama, *penlops* of Bhutan and the kings of Ladakh. The very nature of raising a field force made training an unlikely event. Many matchlock holders did not have the resources to be able to practise and become proficient in their use; shot was poorly made and powder of varying quality. The rate of fire was slow.

Throughout the region open warfare was avoided whenever and wherever possible. In addition close-order fighting rarely occurred. All forces preferred to build defensive positions when facing invaders. Lengthy dry stone walls, rapidly constructed and loopholed, were built across valley floors, defiles and gorges from which matchlocks and jingalls would provide an offensive fire when opportunity presented itself. Usually about 2m (7ft) tall they were notcrenellated but contained two rows of square gun loops running the whole length of the wall, which was frequently reinforced by sangars. Cavalry, regarded as elite troops, usually fought dismounted. This avoidance of man-to-man combat was turned to the advantage of the Gurkhas when the Nepalese army invaded Tibet. Waiting until the matchlock men had discharged their weapons they attacked whilst reloading was taking place; their ferocious, close contact and disciplined fighting routed the Tibetans.

Throughout the whole region large numbers of fortified buildings were constructed over centuries. Paradoxically, protracted sieges were rare occurrences. It is not difficult to see why – the climate is harsh, winters are long and armies had tremendous difficulties in living off the land. In addition, the monumental dzongs and fortress monasteries in many instances served as vast granaries and storehouses for their dependent villages and peasantry. The difficulty in supplying and providing the manpower for a sustained siege was beyond the resources of all but the Chinese and Mongols.

HIMALAYAN FORTIFICATIONS

Generic approaches and the principles of defence

The Tibetan Cultural Region contains many remains of fortifications that have been built over the last 1,000 years or so, sadly most now little more than huge piles of rubble. Although they are of many varying types and forms, three are unique to the region: the huge and unexplained watchtowers of Kham; the dzongs of Tibet and the fortress monasteries of Bhutan. Although the former have been subjected to wanton Chinese destruction, photographic records from the first half of the 20th century together with recorded descriptions give us a good insight into the form they took.

Reputably the oldest existing building in Tibet is the fort of Yumbulagang in the Yarlung Valley, which is believed to have originally been built in the 8th century AD as the seat of the early kings. However, it has been rebuilt over the centuries and was recently severely damaged by the Chinese. The accuracy of the reconstruction is debatable. However, the central lookout tower is similar to many that existed in the southern valleys of Tibet although smaller than the enigmatic towers of Kham, the majority of which date from around the 14th century. These towers are soundly built of uncut stones and many are, intriguingly, star shaped and rise to a height of between 25 and 40m (80–130ft). As well as serving as lookout and defensive towers it is postulated that they were also places of power proclaiming the wealth and status of their owners. Many were attached to the manorial farm

The fortress of the medieval kings of Tibet in the Yarlung Valley, dating from the 8th century AD, has been rebuilt many times. The multistoreyed tower is thought to have served as the template for the many defensive and lookout towers scattered throughout Tibet.

complexes, some of whose residential buildings rose to four storeys.

In Tibet the aristocracy tended to live in the dzongs whilst in the Himalayan areas of Ladakh and Mustang fortress palaces were built. Although most are now ruined a number are found in Ladakh, notably at Shey, Leh, Basgo and Temisgang of which that at Leh is the best preserved. In Tibet, as the fifth Dalai Lama attempted to reunify the country newly subjugated areas were ruled from powerful fortresses, many of which were newly built or enlarged.

Invariably built on the top or crests of huge rocky outcrops these were monumental provincial fortresses, and their numerous towers, walls, barracks, administrative buildings and, occasionally, temples form complexes that totally dominate the surrounding countryside. They overlook and often overshadow their neighbouring monasteries. The only example that has survived of this relationship is seen at Gyantse. The projection of power from the central authority in Lhasa revolved around the close cooperation between lamas and nobility until the time of the fifth Dalai Lama, when one or two *dzongpons* – the 'lord' of the dzong – one frequently a high-ranking monk, exercised local authority from the dzong during a three-year appointment.

The origin of the Tibetan dzong is not known although there is evidence of Chinese and Mongol influences in the style of their military architecture. Early photographs show that some appear to be concentric fortresses, as at Phari on the Tibetan-Sikkim border occupied by Younghusband in 1903. Others had covered ways protected by round towers that led down from the crest to a water source. A particularly fine example, photographed in 1903, was to be found at Khampa dzong, 30km (19 miles) from the Sikkim border. Built on a ridge the dzong dominates the surrounding plains and a covered way leads down to the valley floor where a group of five round towers appear to act as a barbican. Towers are square, rectangular or round and appear to have been crowned with hoarding. Although walls are provided with wall-walks, and rising parapets are stepped, there is no evidence of crenellations on the one remaining dzong or photographs taken over the last 100 years.

Walled towns are rare in the cultural region. Whilst the Potala Palace had a walled monastic village attached to it, and the surrounding town had the remains of its eastern gatehouse, until recently there is no record of any other town in Tibet being walled, although some dzongs had walled villages at their foot, as at Lhatse dzong which guards a river crossing west of Gyantse on the trade route to Kashgar. A similar arrangement was seen in Leh in Ladakh where there was a walled town attached to the king's palace. There were no townships in Bhutan until recently; here the dzongs were large enough to shelter their dependent population. In the north-west of Nepal is the almost unknown ex-kingdom of Mustang. The walled capital of Lo Manthang together with its monasteries and palace is, today, almost unchanged from the 17th century.

Occasionally, walls rising steeply on each side barricaded roads through narrow gorges, defiles or river valleys. These were almost always dry-stone built and hastily erected, although the Younghusband mission came across a magnificent and permanent example at Yatung on the trade route from India; it was designed to control entry into Tibet from Sikkim and serve as a customs post. Superbly constructed, the wall is reinforced with sangars and appears to be crenellated; the merlons are loopholed.

With the resurgence of Buddhism in the 14th and 15th centuries many monasteries were built in the Tibetan Cultural Region, with some being protected by neighbouring dzongs. Others, especially those in remote valleys or in the arid Jang Tang, were vulnerable to looting by brigands and bandits, or attacks by rival monasteries and lineages, warring nobility or by external invaders. The need for defence increased as the number of donations and thus wealth increased. Different regions had different needs reflected in the varying architectural monastic complexes that developed.

In Tibet a fortified perimeter wall enclosed many monasteries that were built in valleys. The earliest monastery that has a fortified appearance is at Samye, not far from Lhasa. Dating from the 7th century AD it still retains its elliptical, metre-thick, perimeter wall stretching over a kilometre in length, and 4m (13ft) tall. Four gates break the wall at cardinal points and are provided with guardrooms.

Many other monasteries, especially those built on trade routes were walled; some with very powerful fortifications as at Chokhorgyel, Litang and Sakya, west of Shigatse. Many, however, relocated – moving into the remotest of places, often on the tops of mountains where access was difficult. Very occasionally a monastery was developed inside the dzong itself. Dechen dzong, guarding the northern approaches to Lhasa is one example that contained a theological college.

In Ladakh and its neighbouring valleys monasteries were built on valley floors, usually in the lee of the castles and forts of the ruling nobility. As in central Tibet the combination of a hilltop fort with a nearby monastery was used to pacify, control and administer newly acquired territory by the kings of Guge, who had forged their kingdom in western Tibet and parts of Ladakh, and their successors the kings of Ladakh. Although now a comparatively poor region, in the 16th to 19th centuries it was wealthy owing to the number of trade routes passing through the region; much of this wealth was donated to the monasteries. The threat from neighbouring Islamic Baltistan to the undefended monasteries was countered by the relocation of nearly all the monasteries. Forts had always been built on easily defended mountaintops and the monastic complexes moved up the mountains to join them and form compact defensible units. Monk architects imitated their military colleagues and built their temples and accommodation and administration buildings upwards. In addition the outer walls of the lower buildings presented a blank façade. Narrow passageways were overlooked by the multi-storeyed buildings they led to. Along with the four fortress palaces they formed a defensive chain that could shelter and protect the dependent villagers, as well as protecting their riches, sacred artefacts and libraries.

This view of Khamba dzong shows the defensive walls that led from the dzong to its water supply in the valley below, which was defended by five round towers. It was impossible to dig wells through the rock of these mountaintop fortresses and there is no evidence that cisterns were built. (Courtesy of National Museums Liverpool)

THE FORTIFIED MONASTERIES OF TIBET

The background

The monastic architecture of Tibet has altered little in form and function over the centuries since the first monastery was built at Samye in the 7th century AD. There is, however, a great variation in size and wealth depending upon lay patronage, donations and land holdings; some becoming, in effect, monastic cities. The great age of monastic building began in the 15th century. From this period the monasteries of Drepung, Sera and Ganden still remain, the 'Three Seats of State' built to the north of Lhasa. Drepung monastery, founded in 1416, had become one of these monastic cities by the time of the fifth Dalai Lama. In its heyday it housed some 10,000 monks engaged in many differing activities. None of these monasteries was fortified although precinct walls surrounded them. Others, especially those in the more remote areas, were much smaller with the monk body often numbering less than a hundred. Although many monasteries were walled, to demarcate the spiritual from the profane, monks were an integral part of Tibetan society and had a close relationship with both their settled and nomadic lay neighbours. Forbidden to own anything but their robes, the Buddhist monks converted their monastic wealth into religious statuary, shrines, reliquary chortens and altars. Such was their wealth by the beginning of the 17th century that the monasteries were known by the Chinese as 'the great storehouses in the west'.

Although a number of monks in each monastery were detailed to act as security guards to protect the monastic riches, things were to change after 1610 when the King of Tsang attacked Sera and Drepung from Shigatse in the west. Religious and civil strife now began in earnest. In response many monasteries sought to protect themselves by converting their boundary walls into powerful fortifications by heightening and widening them and adding corner and interval towers and bastions. In addition many monasteries took on a new function; they were to act as places of refuge. For centuries there were constant threats from the ubiquitous bandits and brigands, outside invaders and aristocratic and lamaistic power struggles. In addition they acted as repositories for the safe keeping of goods and chattels; these functions continued in Kham, in the east, well into the 20th century. This was a symbiotic relationship as it was the donated agricultural surplus and monies obtained from trade that enabled the voluminous monastic communities to devote considerable amounts of time to study, meditation and artistic works.

Despite the titular role of the Dalai Lama as the supreme ruler, his authority was considerably lessened the further away from Lhasa the monasteries

Samye monastery, built on the northern valley floor of the Yarlung Tsangpo (Bramaputra) River, is Tibet's oldest monastery and dates from the 8th century AD. It has endured pillage, fire and earthquake but has always been rebuilt in the same form.

Central southern Tibet

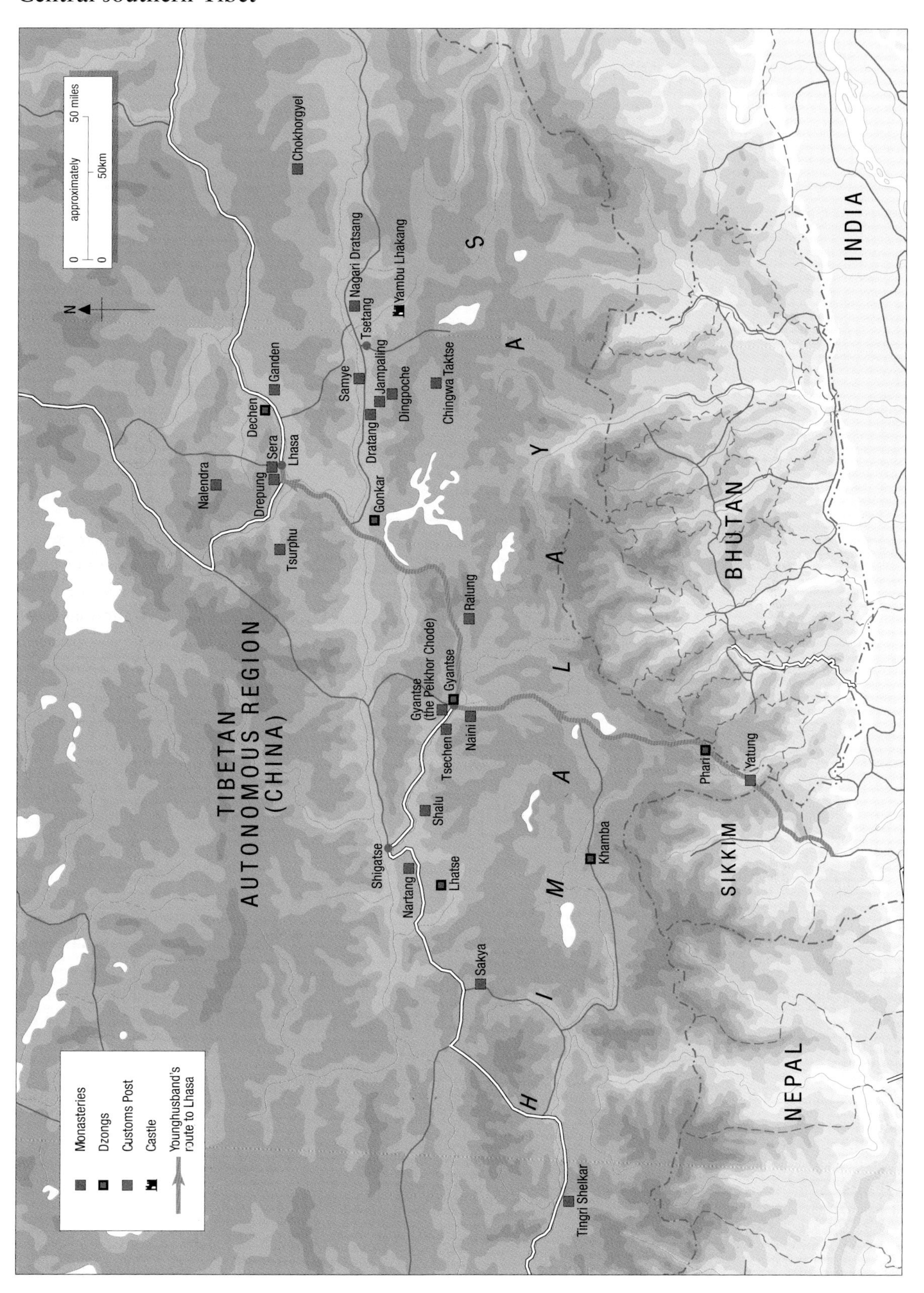

were situated. The immense size of the country (it is seven times the size of Great Britain) made lines of communication tenuous and central authority difficult to enforce. As a consequence the monastic lamas were able to exert considerable political as well as spiritual power and influence in their localities, and many monasteries served as courthouses with lamas acting as intermediaries in civil and legal disputes.

The role that monasteries played in trade has not been studied to any great degree, but that they played an important role is not challenged. The Tibetan Cultural Region has always played a role in the trade between China, India and north and central Asia. In the more remote areas where there were power vacuums and significant degrees of lawlessness, together with a lack of settlements of any size, fortified monasteries and their attendant villages could offer a significant degree of physical security for the trading caravans. It seems likely that they acted in much the same way that the protective fortified caravanserais did to safeguard pilgrims and traders in the neighbouring Islamic counties.

The architectural features of the fortress monasteries, exemplified by the southern monastery at Sakya

One fortified monastery has survived surprisingly intact in the small town of Sakya 130km (80 miles) south-west of Shigatse. The Sakyapa school of Tibetan Buddhism is one of the four main lineages and its seat is here. A monastery was first founded north of the Trum-chu (river), which runs through the town, in 1037. The Patriarch of the Sakyapa school was to become very influential at the Mongolian royal court of Kublai Khan and Tibet was, de facto, ruled from here during the period of Sakyapa hegemony that began in 1268 and lasted for almost 100 years. This coincided with the founding, to the south of the river of another monastic complex, the Chode Lho, within huge defensive walls. Although the northern monastery has been almost totally destroyed, the southern monastery has escaped relatively intact. The huge perimeter wall is 35m (115ft) tall, heavily buttressed, and is some 5m (16ft) thick. It is complete on all four sides enclosing an area over 150m square (1,615 square feet). At each corner there is a rectangular bastion and interval reinforcing towers are found on all four sides; that on the east serving as the (solitary) gate tower. These bastions and towers rise above the enceinte and the wall-walk of the curtain wall that continues through them. Built of mud-brick, its dark grey appearance adds to its imposing strength. In addition there was an outer enceinte, devoid of supporting towers and is only 2–3m (7–10ft) tall today. The Mongolian influence is apparent. Although the dating of Tibetan architecture is difficult, these fortifications are believed to have been built in the 14th century.

The monastery of Sakya escaped the depredations of the PLA and Red Guards. Concentric walls surround the temples and library, although the outer wall is now much lowered. It was built in the 13th century and has remained the principal monastery of the Sakyapa sect since.

Inside its protective walls the monastery still retains much of its spiritual and cultural treasures. The roof of the central temple, the Lhakang Chenmo, is supported by four huge tree trunks richly painted and it houses many chortens containing the embalmed mortal remains of a number of the early abbots. The monastic library is believed to be the largest in Tibet and is thought to contain tens of thousands of Sutras, the Buddhist texts, many saved from the northern monastery prior to its destruction. No other fortress monastery has survived to the same degree.

Chokhorgyel Monastery: the Triune, 'three in one', *gompa*

Founded in 1509 in the Metoktang Valley 160km (100 miles) south-east of Lhasa is a unique fortress monastery differing from Sakya. The monastery here demonstrates how the Tibetans mixed magic, superstition and omens with pragmatic and powerful military architecture. Although the monastic buildings are now ruinous (the Chinese removed all timber during the Cultural Revolution) the huge defensive walls reinforced with bastions and four gateway towers remain arranged in the form of an equilateral triangle; each side is approximately 400m (1,310ft) long.

Founded in 1509 to accommodate pilgrims and lamas on their way to the sacred lake of Lhamo Latso the site is divine. Here three rivers meet, three valleys diverge and three mountains overlook the flat valley plain, upon which the monastery is built; in addition air, water and earth were in balance. Divinity and stout walls, however, were not sufficient to prevent the northern nomadic Dzungar Mongols, despite professing to be Buddhist, from sacking the monastery in 1718 during an interlude on their way to Lhasa.

Dechen dzong

Built on a hill, overlooking the left bank of the Kyi-chu 21km (13 miles) from Lhasa, this ruined dzong was built to guard the northern approaches to the Potala and city. Although most dzongs contained a temple, here was built the Sanghnak Kar – a Buddhist Yellow Hat college of distinction. It escaped destruction only because it was used by the Chinese to store grain in the 1960s. As a consequence it is the only example of its type still in existence and still contains many of its frescos undamaged.

Gyantse – dzongs, monasteries and the British

Gyantse lies 260km (160 miles) from Lhasa and was, until the last century, the third largest town in Tibet. It demonstrates the relationship between dzong and monastery better than anywhere else, despite the depredations firstly of the British and then of the Chinese. The town sits at a crossroads and it controlled, from the medieval period onwards, much of the wool and timber trade.

The town lies in the valley of the Myang-chu and is dominated by a huge dzong dating from the 14th century that occupies almost all of a rocky outcrop and overlooks, but does not overshadow, the neighbouring fortified monastic complex of Pelkhor Chode; built in the lee of a semicircular range of hills to the north it is approximately 500m (1,600ft) distant. Nearby to the south was the fortified manor house of Changlo with the monastery of Naini some 10km (6 miles) away. To the north-west, some 5km (3 miles) distant, on the west bank of the Myang-chu, was the monastery of Tsechen with its accompanying dzong built above it. These served as outposts to the town, monastery and dzong.

The Gyantse dzong

The sole surviving fortress in Tibet that is not ruined, the dzong has undergone recent restoration and is one of the most popular tourist sights in the country. Reputably built in 1268, the hill upon which it was built slopes fairly steeply from the summit to the east and south with almost inaccessible cliff sides to the north and west. As a consequence most of the defences are

The southern approach to Gyantse shows the relationship between the dzong (to the right) and the Pelkhor Chode monastery dwarfed by part of the mighty Himalayan mountain range. In the foreground are stooks of barley and stacks of sun-dried mud-bricks.

RIGHT
This is a view of Gyantse dzong from the south-west in 2001. Although heavily restored in the last 50 years, it was built in the 14th century. From here the kings of Gyantse ruled until the fifth Dalai Lama unified central Tibet in the 17th century. The central building in the foreground contains the 'Memorial Hall of the Anti-British'.

concentrated to the south and east. In 1365 a palace for the governors of Tsang was built on the summit, which is now the citadel containing a temple, the Sampel Rinchenling built at the end of the 14th century, and a lookout tower, open to the elements, that scans the valley in all directions. The upper contours of this rocky outcrop are surrounded by walls and bastions inside of which are a vast number of rooms that served as residences, administrative offices, barracks, an armoury and storerooms. Three walls cut across the slope to the east and a paved road zigzags its way, through three gateways overlooked by protective bastions, to the citadel. In 1903 it was likened by British officers to the rock of Gibraltar.

The fortress monastery of Pelkhor Chode

Also known as Shekar Gyantse, this monastery was founded in 1418 by a prince of Gyantse. It has never belonged to one lineage and, over the centuries,

BOTTOM LEFT
Viewed from the dzong citadel, Pelkhor Chode monastery is slowly being rebuilt.

BOTTOM RIGHT
The Gyantse Kumbum, the golden-domed building to the left, is the only building to survive the destruction carried out by the Chinese apart from the Tanka wall (top right).

A THE FORTRESS MONASTERY OF PELKHOR CHODE, GYANTSE, PRIOR TO ITS DESTRUCTION BY THE CHINESE

The monastery received its fortified enceinte in the late 15th century to shelter its dependent peasantry. Containing the temples and schools of all the various sects, many of its monks took up arms against the Younghusband Expedition. When the nearby dzong was captured it was abandoned to the British.

colleges and schools, the dratsangs, were built for all the sects and many subsects; at its zenith 17 colleges taught here in harmony with each other. After the installation of the fifth Dalai Lama the Gelukpa head lama held the balance of power. Prior to the establishment of these religious schools the Kumbum, a nine-storeyed chorten of 100,000 images of the deities, was completed in 1427. It is almost 40m (130ft) tall, incorporates 75 small chapels and is the largest chorten in Tibet. Surprisingly, along with the assembly hall, it escaped the depredations of the Red Guards. Protective deities guard the entrance and many of the enclosed temples contain murals dating from the 15th century as does the assembly hall.

A huge bastioned perimeter wall built of mud-brick on stone foundations enclosed the monastery. Although in a state of disrepair now, it rises 12m (40ft) to the wall walk, and is 4–5m (13–16ft) thick, with 15 bastions remaining. The southern wall is straight and contains the solitary gateway, relocated to the west of the original entrance gate. Elsewhere these impressive walls follow the contours of the hill. Roughly rectangular, measuring approximately 500 by 300m (1,640 by 980ft) much of the enclosed area is now devoid of any buildings, but even when it contained all its monastic buildings it would have been large enough to shelter the whole civil population of the town. Although overlooked by the neighbouring dzong this is a powerful fortress monastery whose abbot shared power with the *dzongpon*.

Two of the four 'Protective Deities' that guard the entrance to the Kumbum. The temple room housing these fearsome defenders frequently served as the monastic armoury.

The British in Gyantse and the assault on the dzong, 5–6 July 1904

In December 1903 a composite British Indian army, commanded by General James Macdonald, entered Tibet from India by way of Sikkim. Its purpose was to escort a mission, led by Colonel Younghusband. Ostensibly it was to be a peaceful mission designed to neutralize the perceived influence that the Russians had on the Dalai Lama. A more clandestine view was that Britain wanted exclusive trading rights with Tibet. Gyantse was where negotiations were to take place.

Progress was slow and controversial; the slaughter of Tibetans at the pass of Guru, on 31 March 1904, caused consternation in India and London. Fire from two Maxim machine guns manned by a detachment of the Norfolk regiment and disciplined volleys from the Lee-Metfords of Sikh and Gurkha soldiers led to the death of about 340 and the wounding of a further 150 Tibetans from a peasant militia armed only with swords, bows and arrows, and Himalayan matchlocks. When Gyantse was reached the advance stalled. Although Tibetan forces did not occupy the dzong, General Macdonald declined to garrison the fortress. He did, however, have the south-eastern outer walls pulled down and the main, outer,

Taken in 1903 by F. M. Bailey, a mounted infantry officer who accompanied the Younghusband Expedition, this photograph bears the caption 'Monastery and Cho-ten seen enroute to Gyantse'. It depicts, however, part of the relieving column passing the fortress monastery of Naini just south of Gyantse. At the time Tibetan forces had not occupied it. (Courtesy of National Museums Liverpool)

gateway blown up. The manor house and attached farm that belonged to the Tibetan noble family of Changlo was chosen as the mission headquarters. It was fortified with a loopholed perimeter wall and further protected by an abattis, palisade and barbed wire erected by the pioneer corps. For a time Younghusband, with a reduced field force was confined to the environs of the walled manor house. It was approximately 1,300m (4,260ft) from the dzong, from where the Tibetans kept up a persistent, if ineffectual, fire with jingalls and the few pieces of artillery that Tibet possessed. These had been sent from Lhasa.

A relieving field force had to pass the fortified monastery of Naini to the south of the mission post at Changlo. Built on the valley floor the monastery was surrounded by a bastioned wall some 10m (33ft) tall. In addition two small forts were built to defend the high ground behind the monastery and a number of nearby villages were occupied and fortified. In all, the Tibetan defenders here numbered around 900 fighters. Pounded by artillery and assaulted by the 40th Pathans and 8th Gurkhas, all the defended buildings were captured on 25 June. Strengthened by reinforcements, General Macdonald decided to assault and capture Gyantse dzong which had been occupied by thousands of Tibetans. Traditionally and historically, the dzong was regarded as the key to central Tibet and its loss would be very demoralizing for the Tibetans. First, however, another fortified monastery had to be captured. Tsechen monastery occupied the steep southern slope of a precipitous hill that rose 600m (1,970ft) above the river plain to the north-west of Gyantse and overlooked the Gyantse–Shigatse road. The monastic buildings were surrounded by a wall over 3m (10ft) tall and they were further protected to the west by a neighbouring dzong. Approximately 1,000 Tibetan militiamen defended the two fortifications. Bombarded by artillery, both fell to assault and, after the systemic looting of Buddhist artefacts, they were fired and blown up. Thus communications with western Tibet were opened giving access for foraging parties to the fertile Shigatse Valley and its farms.

The way was now open for the mountain batteries to bombard the fort and effect a breach in the south-eastern defences. The walls of the dzong proved durable and it took over 12 hours, using explosive shells, before an assault could be launched. One shell hit a powder magazine which exploded sapping Tibetan resistance. The storming party was composed of soldiers of the Royal Fusiliers and the 8th Gurkhas. The more nimble Gurkhas were first to the breach and their commander Lieutenant John Duncan Grant and Havildar Karbir Pun led them into the interior of the dzong where resistance evaporated. Grant was awarded the Victoria Cross and Pun the Indian Order of Merit 1st Class. The following day General Macdonald led a strong force towards the

Pelkhor Chode, which was considered by the British to be a considerable fortification and believed to be garrisoned by 2,000 Tibetans. After the fall of the dzong the Tibetans had abandoned the monastery and its only occupants were a handful of British officers looting sacred Buddhist objects. Looting from the monasteries around Gyantse proved very contentious. Soldiers were forbidden to loot, but many did. A blind eye was turned towards officers, however, and on occasions looting was officially sanctioned for the benefit of British museums short of Buddhist artefacts. The dzong has been restored and now contains a museum, the 'Memorial Hall of the Anti-British', which certainly lives up to its name. The road to Lhasa was now open and the mission, with its substantial escorting field force, left for the capital on 14 July.

Photographed in 1904, the entrance to Lhasa was through the chorten in the centre, the route taken by Younghusband's forces.

The Potala: the holy palace in the snow land

In 1642 Gushri Khan defeated the King of Tsang ensuring that the Gelukpas would become the dominant Buddhist lineage. In the dzong at Gyantse he bestowed the title of fifth Dalai Lama upon Nagawang Lobsang Gyatso, then a 25-year-old lama, but limited his powers to religious matters. Secular rule remained with Gushri who had installed Sangye Gyatso as his regent or *Desi*.

Although these two held supreme power they lacked physical security in the undefended Drepung monastery. The neighbouring Dechen dzong was too

A very similar view taken in 2001. The chorten and neighbouring buildings have been demolished. Fortunately the Potala is unchanged.

B THE STORMING OF GYANTSE DZONG, LATE AFTERNOON 6 JULY 1904

When General Macdonald decided to assault the fort he anticipated approximately 250 casualties. In the event the dzong was captured with less than an eighth of the expected losses. This was down to four factors. A feigned attack on the north-west of the dzong the previous evening had drawn many of the 2,000 Tibetan defenders away from the south-east defences where the two 10-pdr mountain guns opened a breach between two towers. In addition an explosion in one of the fort's powder magazines resulted in a marked slackening in defensive fire and the order to attack was given. The agility, determination and bravery of the Gurkhas, coupled with the accuracy of the mountain gunners who kept firing at the defenders until the attackers were within 20m (70ft) of the breach enabled the Gurkhas to enter the fort when the remaining defenders fled.

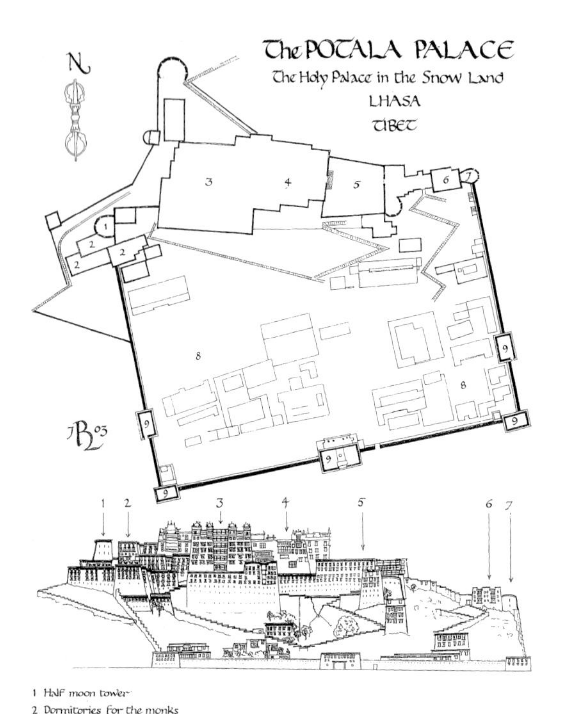

Plan of the Potala Palace.

small for their requirements and the imposing Gongar dzong too far away from the seat of their power at Drepung and the neighbouring Sera and Ganden monasteries. A site was located at Lhasa, then little more than a village, and only 3km (2 miles) south-west of Sera.

Lying in the middle of the river valley of the Kyi-chu at a height of 3,660m (12,000ft) was Mont Marpori approximately 150m (500ft) above the river. The mount was a revered place, the site of a fortification built a millennium earlier for the early kings of Tibet, with a spiritual significance as 'the place where Avalokitesvara lives'. Having determined that this was a propitious site favoured by the Gods and rid of earth demons, building began under the supervision of the *Desi* in 1645. The White Palace, built on the highest part of the mountain was completed in 1653. Over 7,000 labourers and 1,000 artisans and artists, from Tibet, China and Nepal worked on this monumental building. Although incomplete the Dalai Lama thought it prudent to move here in 1648 and it became his residence and administrative centre.

Built in the typical Tibetan manner, it combined the role of monastery, palace and dzong together with offices for Gushri's regent. Only earth, stone and wood were used in its construction. To protect the families of their administrators and bodyguards, the southern slope of Mount Marpori and the flat ground at its bottom were enclosed in a defensive wall 20m (65ft) tall, reinforced with corner bastions and interval towers: that in the middle of the southern wall served as the main gateway. These are of four storeys, the upper two containing windows in typical Tibetan style. There is some similarity to the earlier walls and bastions at Sakya. This enclosed area contained the offices of the lay administration, accommodation blocks, printing presses, a barracks, stables, storehouses and granaries together with lodgings for guests. The eastern and western walls run up the steep sides of Marpori to two huge fortified towers that were built at each edge of the mountain crest. That at the west is 'D' shaped and is known as the moon tower;

One of the corner bastions of the fortified Potala village.

to the east is the round sun tower, attached to which is a rectangular bastion which became a prison for high-ranking dissidents. Between these two towers were built the Namgyal monastery and its monastic cells, the White Palace and its temples together with its external courtyard protected by the round 'Tiger's Lair' tower. On a spur to the north was a fourth tower, now part of the recently constructed road. Thus there were four towers at the cardinal points of the Potala.

Part of the curtain wall, the sun tower and the prison for high-ranking dissidents.

The Great Fifth increasingly took on a secular role from 1658 and soon assumed the role of absolute ruler, thus establishing a theocracy. He died in 1682 and, although he had extended the area over which he ruled, he was unable to unite Tibet in the way the earlier kings had. The *Desi* concealed his death from his subjects, and continued to add to the Potala by building the Red Palace adjacent to the White. The choosing of the next incarnation of the Dalai Lama would be a lengthy process and he feared that the political situation would be destabilized. The building of the Red Palace is believed to have commenced in 1690. Its function was to be spiritual. Containing many temples it also is home to the reliquary chortens of the Great Fifth and the seventh, eighth, ninth and 13th Dalai Lamas. The individual chortens are sheathed in gold and studded with precious stones; that of the Great Fifth rises 20m (65ft) through three storeys and is, reputably, covered with 400kg (880lb) of gold.

The Potala Palace is one of the world's most magnificent buildings. In places it dazzles in colour both internally and externally. The 1,000 or so rooms, connected by labyrinthine passages and reached by stairs that are often no more than ladders, are said to contain over 200,000 images. Walls everywhere are covered in paintings depicting Buddhist imagery and embroidered wall hangings. These artefacts were the work of Tibetan, Nepalese and Chinese artists and craftsmen.

Rising through 13 storeys to a height of over 115m (380ft), it was until recent times one of the tallest and most imposing buildings in the world. It measures 360m (1,180ft) east to west and 335m (1,100ft) north to south.

Externally the Potala changes its mood depending on the weather and is best seen in sunshine when the white and red buildings with their golden roofs

C NEXT PAGE: THE POTALA PALACE, LHASA

Rising majestically from the Lhasa Valley – the 'Land of the Gods' – the appearance of the Potala has altered little over the centuries since its completion at the end of the 17th century depicted here. Designed to perform a multifunctional role (palace, fortress, monastery, administrative centre, storehouse and treasury) the powerful fortifications were necessary to protect the Gelukpa hierarchy and its leader, the Dalai Lama. It was built near the unfortified monastic cities of Drepung and Sera. Built to over awe and demonstrate Gelukpa power and permanence, its fortress role ended in the mid-18th century although it has attracted the devotion of millions of Buddhist pilgrims over the centuries. No longer home to the Dalai Lama, the Potala has become a museum and tourist attraction.

The inset shows the west gate into Lhasa that passed through a chorten or shrine known locally as the Pargo Kaling. The British expeditionary force, under Younghusband entered Lhasa on 6 September 1904. The Chinese have demolished it in recent times.

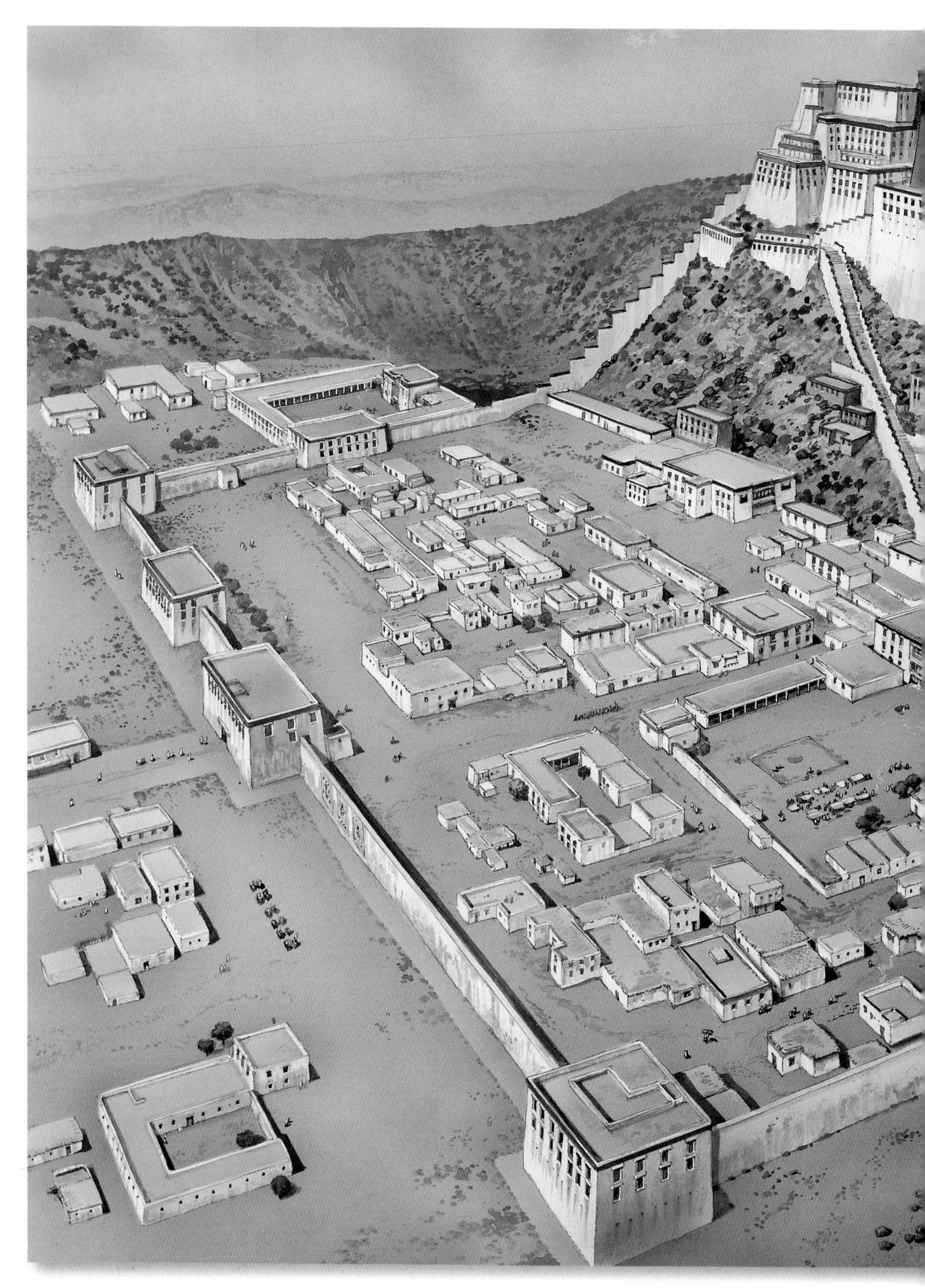

shimmer. This is a powerful place even now and is the embodiment of Tibetan culture. It is rivalled as the most imposing example of religious architecture only by the Vatican in Rome and the now-defunct Palace of the Popes in Avignon. It is the ultimate fusion of monastery and fortress and is substantially unaltered since it was first built. It dominated every aspect of Tibetan life until the voluntary exile of the 14th Dalai Lama in 1959.

It was attacked and captured twice in the 18th century by the Dzungar Mongols, first in 1705 and again in 1717. In addition the People's Liberation Army shelled it during the 1959 uprising. The southern façade, the porch of the Red Palace and the Potala's school were damaged. Fortunately the intervention of Zhou Enlai prevented further destruction.

Where the *Desi* got his inspiration from to build such a magnificent building is unknown. It has been suggested that the dzong at Shigatse and the nine-storey palace in Leh, built a number of decades earlier, were influential. On the Ladakhi border with the Tibetan Autonomous Region is the fortified monastery of Hanle, built under the patronage of King Senge Namgyal before the Potala was started. It has more than a passing resemblance to the Potala. In addition, when the 14th Dalai Lama left Lhasa he spent some time at Lhatse dzong claiming that it reminded him of the Potala.

THE FORTRESS MONASTERIES AND MONASTIC PALACE FORTRESSES OF LADAKH

Ladakh is now a region of the north-western Indian state of Jammu and Kashmir. Straddling both the Karakoram mountain range to the north and the western Himalayas to the south, the sacred Indus River and its valley separate the two ranges. It is a dry and mainly barren region where only the Indus Valley and its tributaries can be cultivated. Although always sparsely populated, until recently it had great strategic importance as it served as a crossroads for the major trading routes between Kashmir and Tibet; as a consequence it received significant revenues, especially in the 17th and 18th centuries. It has been part of the Tibetan Cultural Region for over a millennium and has always been staunchly Buddhist.

By the 11th century Ladakh had its capital at Shey. Buddhist control and conversion followed the Tibetan pattern used so successfully in unifying that country; the symbiotic union of fortress and monastery in Ladakh resulted in

Most of the fortifications of Shey are now ruinous with only fragments remaining. From the citadel only fragments of the defensive walls of the old capital remain. There are, however, many examples of the triangular loopholes common in Ladakhi fortifications.

Below the citadel is the monastic temple cared for over the centuries with the adjacent ruins of a late medieval palace.

political and religious control of the region. Military occupation and conversion went hand in hand. By the end of that century it has been calculated that 108 monasteries with their estates and dependent villages were in existence, protected by neighbouring fortifications. Whilst monasteries were built on the valley floor the fort was always built on high ground.

The Islamic conquests of southern Asia saw the rulers of Ladakh seeking religious, spiritual and physical succour from Tibet in the 15th century. As a result Tibetan Buddhist influence and the Tibetan way of life have been followed until recent times. The 15th-century conversion of Kashmir to Islam proved to be a serious threat to Ladakh. Despite repeated raids, attacks and an invasion from its Islamic neighbours, the region acted as a Buddhist bulwark against Islamic expansionist aims in the western Himalayas for centuries; Buddhists and Muslims became implacable enemies. In addition the increasing wealth and accessibility of the Ladakhi monasteries acted as magnets for raiding war parties and they proved indefensible.

The Ladakhis and their Tibetan advisers, who had the dubious benefit of 200 years of sectarian conflict, came up with a simple and pragmatic solution. Monastery and fort would become one. Defensive considerations dictated that the fort should remain on high ground; it was necessary for the monastery to move, with the fort incorporating the monastic temples, treasures and its monks. As a result, by the 16th century, there was a fusion of the two forms throughout Ladakh.

Today only one example of the separation of fort and monastery remains; at Alchi, 65km (40 miles) downstream from the Ladakhi capital at Leh. The monastery was founded in the 11th century on the south bank of the Indus in a verdant oasis in a desert landscape and contains many important wall paintings, amongst the oldest in Ladakh. The survival of the buildings and murals is believed to be a consequence of the cessation of worship here in the 15th century.

The Namgyal Dynasty

After the catastrophic invasions from Islamic Kashmir in the first half of the 16th century a devastated Ladakh had to be rebuilt. As well as impoverishment and monastic destruction, the country had lost its unity and it had divided into

RIGHT
On top of the crest that overlooks the modern town of Leh are buildings from three different periods. To the left is the 17th-century palace of Sennge Namgyal whilst to the right is the fort and monastery of Namgyal Tsemo, built almost a century earlier; the building painted red-madder is the monastery with the fort above. In between are the ruins of a fortified tower of indeterminate age.

two kingdoms – upper Ladakh with dual capitals at Shey and Leh and the lower kingdom based on Basgo and Temisgang. These four townships were the only settlements of any population size. The Buddhist spirit had not been crushed, however, and the philosophical acceptance of impermanence resulted in over two centuries of reconstruction, often on a monumental scale for such a small kingdom.

Tashi Namgyal reunified the kingdom in the second half of the 16th century and built the fort and monastery of Namgyal Tsemo on a peak above the town at Leh, as well as the monastery of Phiyang 15km (9 miles) to the west of Leh. Despite the efforts of his successors this progress was impeded by the invasion of Ali Mir from neighbouring Baltistan, which caused the devastation of the country once again. Reconstruction had to be restarted and was to reach its zenith during the reign of Sengge Namgyal, the 'lion king', who ruled between *c.*1616 and 1642.

Sengge not only undertook a massive building campaign, both secular and religious, but also expanded the boundaries of his kingdom incorporating the sparsely populated valleys of Zanskar, Spiti and Lahaul. He also annexed parts of Guge in western Tibet to his unified kingdom. All were remote Buddhist regions and contained isolated monasteries.

The fortress monasteries of the 17th century

Almost all of the fortress monasteries that are found today in Ladakh date from the time of Sengge. As elsewhere in the Tibetan Cultural Region the great majority have undergone numerous reconstructions, but it is possible to detect the form they took when first built.

All were built on isolated hills, on crags or on rocky outcrops. The style is recognizably Tibetan and the majority were multistoreyed, with temples occupying the uppermost storeys. Openings are few and increase in size only in the upper levels where they are provided with wooden balconies. The high, sloping walls are painted white externally; below

BELOW
The monastery of Chemrey rises for seven storeys from the pinnacle of an isolated hill in the Indus Valley. Below it are the secular buildings of the monastery's dependents with the monastic estates below in the Indus Valley. The richness of a monastery was proportionate to the extent of the estates it controlled.

these fortified temple complexes are ranged, tier upon tier, the cells of monks and their educational and domestic buildings. Narrow labyrinthine alleys make access to the temples difficult, with the buildings huddling close together. The massive bulk of the monastic temples, together with assembly and prayer rooms, combined with their carefully chosen locations still create the impression of powerful fortifications even though their active defences have been removed or lost. Many were provided with outlying lookout towers to give advance warning of danger. The lay peasantry lived in small villages and tended the monastic estates and their own fields supporting the monastery materially with gifts and labour. In return the monastery gave spiritual and administrative guidance and provided a refuge when danger threatened.

Reputedly the earliest of Sengge's fortress monasteries was that of Spituk, 15km (9 miles) west of Leh. Unfortunately its name, which means 'effective as an example' cannot be verified as it lies within an Indian army encampment that guards Leh airfield.

The monasteries at Chemry and Hanle

The monastery at Chemry perhaps best typifies the appearance of the 17th-century fortress monasteries. Perched on top of an isolated hill overlooking its estates, the monastery is situated on one side of a tributary valley of the Indus approximately 45km (30 miles) south-east of Leh. Straddling one side of the hill are the monastic domestic buildings and the monastic fortress crowns a visually pleasing complex. Although believed to be one of Sengge's foundations it was most likely built in 1644 as a 'funeral act of merit' for him.

Much further to the south-east, over 200km (125 miles) from Leh is the fortified monastery of Hanle. Built on a crest in the Zanskar mountain range, at a height of 4,600m (15,000ft), by Sengge it has always belonged to the Red Hat Drukpa sect. Now in a sensitive backwater of India, only 20km (12 miles) from the border with Tibet, it played a very important role when first built as it was a major staging post on the lucrative *pashm* (cashmere wool) Kashmiri–Lhasa trading route.

Sengge spent a considerable amount of time here, prior to moving to the palace he built at Leh, after he had relocated the Ladakhi capital to the town. It was at Hanle that he died in 1642 after he had taken a Ladakhi army into Tibet to confront the Mongols who had occupied Tsang in western Tibet and were threatening his kingdom.

The monastery is one of the largest in Ladakh and is very reminiscent of the Potala Palace in Lhasa, which was built later, although it is smaller and much more austere. The sharply pointed ridge was enlarged by two infilled retaining walls to provide a platform for the two-storey building that housed the temples, *gonkhang* and assembly halls of the Drukpas. As at the Potala, two defensive walls run down the southern side of the crest. Both the parapets and wall-walks are stepped and reinforced with interval and corner towers; that to the west is round and contains box machicolations as does the solitary square gatehouse tower in the middle of the loopholed wall that runs between the two corner towers.

The defensive system in the Ladakhi Indus Valley

The majority of Ladakhis lived in the fertile Indus Valley between Khaltse in the north-west and Upshi in the south-west. It was at these two villages that the trans-Himalayan routes, from Kashmir and the Punjab respectively, entered the broad and fertile valley. The distance between the two villages is

The restored, stone-built, monastic citadel overlooks the rest of the fortress of Basgo and is separated from the late medieval mud-brick palaces by a gulley.

approximately 120km (75 miles) and the valley contains all the main centres of population together with all the important monasteries, known in Ladakh as *gompas*, outside Zanskar.

Although the remote valley *gompas* were left to their own devices to protect themselves and their dependent villages this was not the case in the Ladakhi Indus Valley. The string of fortress monasteries that ran from Lamayuru in the north-west, just outside Khaltse, to Chemrey near Upshi became part of a defensive system developed over the 16th and first half of the 17th centuries to safeguard the valley population. This was to reach its zenith in the 1630s with the building of the multistoreyed palace fortress at Leh. Other palace fortresses existed at Shey, Basgo and Temisgang. These palace complexes also contained not only temples but their attendant monastic buildings. Each followed a similar architectural template, although their internal spatial arrangements differed; Basgo, for example, incorporates the largest fortress temple and Leh the largest fortified palace. In addition, walled towns were attached at Leh and Temisgang whilst at Shey an artificial lake added to the defences.

Interspaced were the fortress monasteries of Mulbekh, Lamayuru, Ridzong, Likir, Phiyang, Spituk, Tiske, Matho, Stakna, Hemis and Chemrey; most built on isolated, steep-sided hills. Crowning the high points of the valley sides, and sometimes at the entrance to tributary valleys, were lookout towers. The building costs of the defensive system, in time, labour and money, were very high and achieved only by a population committed to the Tibetan Buddhist way of life together with finances raised by the merchant class and custom dues. There is contemporary evidence for this; towards the end of the 16th century Diogo d'Almeida, a Portuguese merchant who visited Ladakh and stayed for two years, recorded that the country was rich and opulent.

The fortified temple, monastery and palace complex at Basgo

This defensive site is superb. A huge spur from the valley's northern mountainous walls encroaches to such a degree that the Indus Valley is almost cut in two. The spur ended abruptly near the river, resulting in unscalable cliff walls to east, south and west. Rising fairly steeply to the north, the spur is transected by a shallow gorge separating it from its higher northern part.

The building history of the fortified complex has not been recorded but inspection reveals building techniques of different styles, materials and periods. The present-day appearance suggests that the southern pinnacle was fortified with a series of walls, towers and buildings that followed its irregular contour, giving what appears to be, in parts, a double layer of fortifications overlooking the valley road, the river and the lay settlement. These can be traced with certainty only to the south-west as much of the southern cliff wall is covered in the rubble of collapsed buildings. To the west of this is a palace, probably dating from the 18th or 19th century. Some of the fortifications that still stand are well built, with rows of large, rough-cut square stones separated by three to four layers of much thinner stone.

The southernmost building within the complex is the Ser-Zangs (gold and copper) temple dating from the 17th century. Two storeys high it contains an image of the future Buddha three storeys tall; his head projects above the ceiling of the top storey of the temple and is enclosed within a glazed and ornamented box-like structure. Immediately to the north of the temple are the much-ruined, wind-eroded remains of three royal fortified palaces built out of mud-brick. Separated from them by the depression to the north is a huge temple, the Chamba Lhakhang, built by one of the earlier Namgyal kings in the middle of the 16th century. Although this temple also acted as a keep or citadel, it contains a clay, copper and gilt Maitreya image, rising through three storeys, together with important murals from the period. After Alchi it is probably the most beautifully painted temple in Ladakh. Reputedly this temple-keep could be reached only by a covered way from the part of the fortress complex containing the palaces, which acted themselves as the inner bailey. A number of ruined and isolated large towers lie some distance from the complex, all built on rocky pinnacles of the spur. Whether those to the west and south were ever connected to each other or the fortified complex by a curtain wall is not known.

Much of Basgo is now in ruins but it is understandable how it was never taken. The defences in a number of places appear concentric and complex.

As with many fortified buildings in the Tibetan Cultural Region the source of the water supply is unknown. What is known is that in 1680, on the orders of the Great Fifth from his Potala Palace, a combined Tibetan and Mongol army invaded Ladakh and defeated its army at the approaches to the Chang La mountain pass. The remnants of the Ladakhi army fled to Basgo where they occupied the fortress. Besieged for three years they held out until relieved

On another isolated rocky hill, on the southern bank of the Indus lies the monastery of Matho. It is the only Gompa belonging to the Sakyapas in Ladakh and was part of the defensive system of the Indus Valley.

by an Islamic army from Kashmir. Following the Tibetan pattern, huge stores of grain and other foodstuffs had been stored at Basgo but where the source of the apparent perennial water supply came from has not been discovered.

The fortress palace of Sengge Namgyal at Leh

The finest secular building in Ladakh was built in Leh in the mid 1630s by Sengge Namgyal as his palace. Built, like the palaces at Shey and Basgo, at the southern end of a mountain spur it looms over and dominates the town that lies at its foot. The rectangular palace is nine storeys tall and has the aura of a fortress, although it has served as the palace of the royal family until recent times.

Why Sengge built his palace here is open to speculation. Certainly Shey is a more strategic site and had been strongly fortified long before Leh received its city wall. It has been postulated that towards the end of Sengge's reign Leh's position as a trading town had eclipsed all the other towns in the Indus Valley, particularly Shey. In addition there was a comparatively peaceful environment. This mighty fortress palace exudes power even now, and remains a visual statement of the power and wealth of Ladakh's most famous king.

Built of well-coursed field stone in a mud mortar, the palace is nine storeys tall on its south and eastern aspect with the lower two storeys devoid of any external openings. Measuring approximately 100 by 50m (330 by 165ft) the solitary entrance is via a porticoed doorway into its eastern wall. All four walls slope inward and are massively buttressed. The openings at each floor level are neatly arranged one above another. Those at the lowest levels are very narrow, little more than loopholes but increase in size as the floors rise; many of the window-sized openings of the top four storeys are provided with wooden balconies. Nearly all the openings face east with a few to the south. Both these sides are surrounded by buildings of two to four storeys, rising up in tiers from the town. They appear contemporaneous with the fortress palace and almost all of their outer façades are blank apart from narrow loophole-type openings. Like all buildings in Ladakh they are flat roofed.

The architect and architectural precedents are unknown; certainly no other secular building rises to the same height and it is rivalled in its enormity only by one or two of the largest valley monasteries. The palace is recorded as being built in three years and completed a number of years before the

The ruined palace of the 'Lion King' at Leh was not only a powerful fortress but was surrounded by a circuit of buildings that was also fortified. Although the buildings served different functions the contiguous blank outer façades were loopholed and provided additional defences.

king's death. Thus, along with his monastery at Hanle, it pre-dates the Potala Palace. Their architectural influences are striking.

The hidden valleys of Zanskar, Lahaul and Spiti

Over the centuries of its existence the geographical extent of the kingdom of Ladakh reached its zenith during the reign of Sengge when he incorporated Guge and the remote and high valleys of Zanskar, Lahaul and Spiti. These three neighbouring regions have always been staunchly Buddhist and their mountain fastness ensured that outside influence, other than from Lhasa was minimal.

Zanskar: the 'land of white copper' and the fortified monastery of Bardan

The river Zanskar, formed by the confluence of the Stod and Lingnak rivers, joins the Indus near Basgo. Until recently access to the valley was by mountain passes – through the Zanskar range to the north and the western part of the great Himalayan range to the south, and then only for four summer months before snow closed them. It is one of the most remote and highest inhabited valleys in the world at a mean altitude of around 4,000m (13,120ft) and is approximately 300km (190 miles) long. The first European to visit the valley was Csoma de Koros in 1823; a Hungarian by birth he is regarded as being 'the father of Tibetology'.

Both the Drukpa and Gelukpa schools have adherents here and each possesses four monasteries. Of the eight, only Sani was built on flat ground, the remainder being built on the sides or crests of mountains with only the monastery of Bardan being fortified. Founded in the early years of the 17th century it overlooks the left bank of the river Lingnak 12km (7 miles) downriver from the Zanskar capital of Padum.

Built on top of an isolated rocky outcrop with seemingly unassailable cliff sides this Drukpa Kagyupa *gompa* perches 100m (325ft) above the river. Commanding the river valley, it always performed a military role as well as a religious one. Access is via a climbing and winding path cut into the rock face with only a narrow landing in front of the solitary entrance. As at a number of other Himalayan monasteries (cf. Hanle), the surface area of the narrow summit was enlarged with tall infilled retaining walls on which the monastery was built. The appearance is of an austere and powerful fortress. Built of stone the monastic buildings rise in four tiers to the three-storey temple built on the rocky peak. The monastic buildings enclose a courtyard and shelter it from the harsh winter climate. The site of this fortress monastery has always been strategic and was further protected by a fort, now ruined, on an overlooking peak. It has been besieged and sacked on a number of occasions and was, allegedly, looted by Pakistani soldiers during the troubles of partition in 1947.

The fortress monasteries of Spiti

Both Lahaul and Spiti are now districts in the Indian state of Himachal Pradesh to the south of Ladakh. Although distinct valleys they are connected by the Kunzum pass. The landscape is typical mountain desert; both share a harsh climate and Spiti is the more barren of the two. Eleven old monasteries are found in the two valleys but only in Spiti is there evidence today that they served as fortress monasteries. Located 12km (7 miles) from Kaza, the capital, is Key *gompa*, the largest monastery in Spiti. It was built as a fortress monastery on top of and around the sides of a steep conical hill although its appearance has changed over the centuries. It became a Gelukpa monastery after it was captured in the seventeenth century by a Mongol army on the orders of the Great Fifth. During the nineteenth it was attacked and sacked by Dogras and Sikhs. In addition it was ravaged by fire in the 1840s and damaged by an earthquake in 1975. As a consequence the reconstructed buildings have lost their defensive role with low buildings cascading down the hill-sides haphazardly; only the hilltop temples retain a fortified air.

The 15th-century Dankar monastery (its name translates as 'fort on a cliff'), lies between Kaza and Tabo and crowns a 300m-tall (980ft) spur that juts out into the valley and overlooks the confluence of the Spiti and Pin rivers. A number of multistoreyed buildings rise to the pinnacle of the spur. It was built to serve three roles: monastery, place of refuge and as a lookout and warning post to guard the valley.

Two further monasteries are fortified and, rarely for the high Himalayas, were built on the valley floor. The monastery at Tangyud, 4km (21/2 miles) from Kaza, was built on the edge of a canyon and is surrounded by walls which appear to have been influenced by the fortress monastery of Sakya in Tibet. This is not surprising as Tangyud was built in the first quarter of the fourteenth century and has always belonged to the Sakyapa sect.

The oldest monastery in the western Himalayan region is that at Tabo, believed to have been founded at the end of the 10th century. Surrounded by high mud-brick defensive walls, the monastery contains nine temples, many of which are decorated with murals showing a definite Indian influence.

NEPAL

The hidden Kingdom of Mustang and the fortified town of Lo Manthang

Mustang, now part of Nepal after its annexation at the end of the 18th century, was formerly the independent Kingdom of Lo. It is almost totally surrounded by Tibet, which has influenced its culture and history closely. It is peopled by the Lobas who are related both culturally and ethnically to the Tibetans living in the centre and west of Tibet, with whom they share a common language.

Bisected by the upper reaches of the Kali Gandaki River, its high altitude and arid landscape have ensured that its population has always been low and yet, between the 15th and 17th centuries, this tiny kingdom played an important role in the trade between Tibet and Central Asia to the north and India to the south, controlling one of the easiest routes from the southern plains to the Tibetan plateau. Trade developed in both directions; Yak caravans carried salt and goat, sheep and Yak wool from Tibet and returned with grain for the northern nomads, spices and manufactured goods.

Buddhism, in the form of the Sakyapa School, had been introduced in the early part of the 15th century. Following the Tibetan pattern, monasteries were established along the river valley and its tributaries together with their dependent villages and protective forts. Whilst a number of the former still function, almost all of the latter are now ruined.

The capital has always been at Lo Manthang, 'the southern plains of aspiration', and it still retains the medieval character and appearance of its founding. Its population rarely exceeded a thousand Lobas and its protective ramparts have sheltered three monasteries, a royal palace, and over 100 two- or three-storey houses for centuries; the latter are for the Mustang nobility. The ramparts are, in comparison with the houses, massive. Six metres (20ft) tall and 3m (10ft) thick in places, they are built of rammed earth and mud-

The dzongs of Bhutan

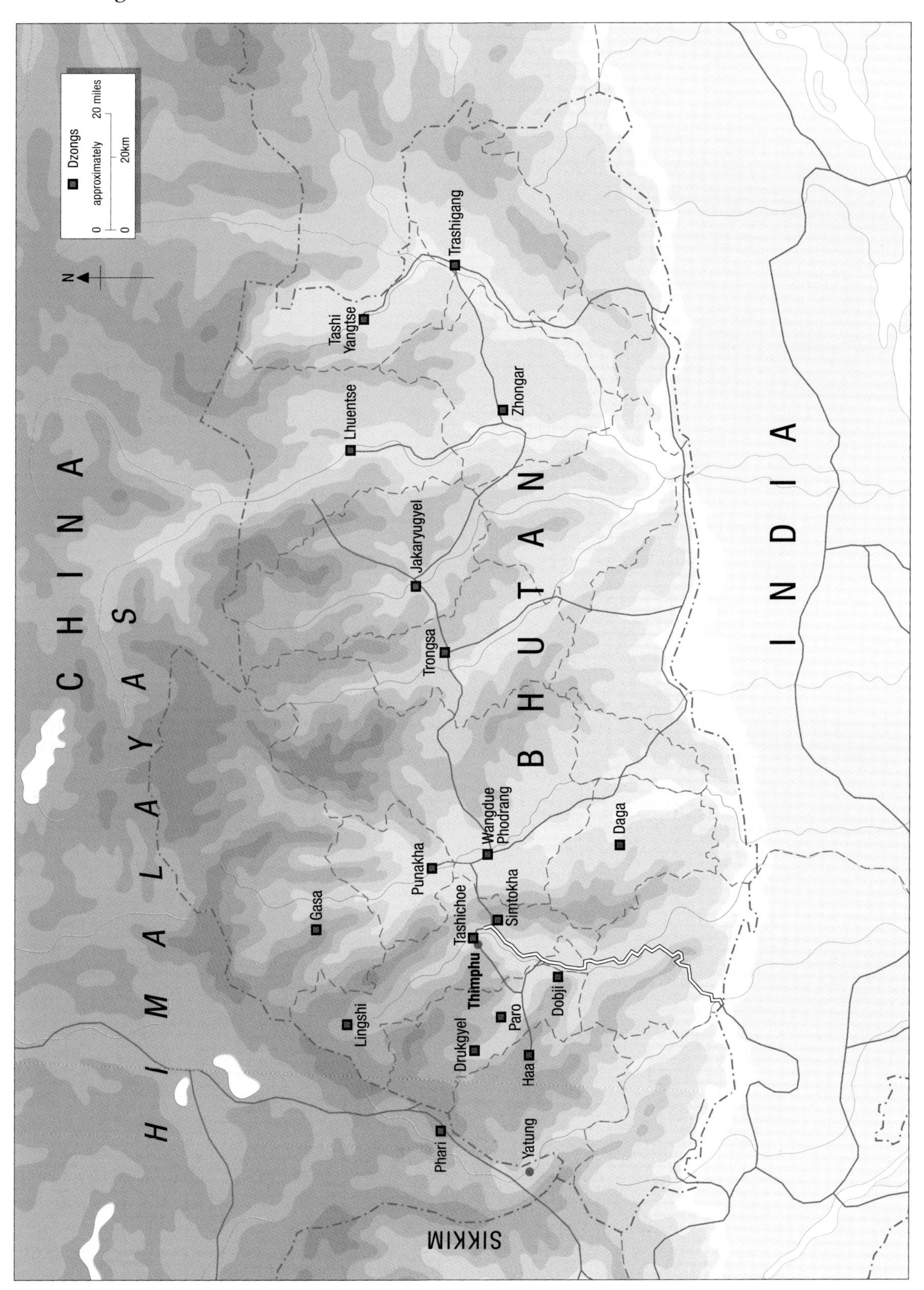

brick, although the tower that contains the solitary gateway in the northern wall is built of river boulders in a mud mortar. Rectangular bastions reinforce the walls, together with interval towers, throughout the old town as well as in the additional town enclosure to the north-west. The old town walls measure approximately 160m (525ft) north to south and 145m (475ft) east to west. Most of the houses, the royal palace and two of the monasteries lie within these ramparts, together with a number of chortens of differing sizes. Many of the houses surround small courtyards and in a number of instances the alleyways run under the houses at ground-floor level.

The five-storey royal palace is believed to date from the end of the 17th century and is a scaled-down copy of that built in Leh. It dominates the solitary gateway. To the west of the palace are two monasteries of a much earlier date. The grandest, the Tupchen Lhakhang, contains a magnificent assembly hall and a tower that is the tallest building in Lo Manthang; its red walls are visible from far away and act as a beacon for travellers. It also contains a huge Maitreya statue. The monastery dates from the early 1470s. Next to it is the 'Mustang God House', another red-painted monastery which was founded in 1448.

Around the first quarter of the 18th century the king commissioned a third monastery, the Choeda or 'New *gompa*'. There was no space available in the town and it was built outside to the north-west. The western wall was extended and further defensive walls built to enclose the monastic ensemble. In addition, houses were built to accommodate the overspill population and provide the only open space of any size for Buddhist festivals. This added enceinte measures 120 by 90m (390 by 295ft). As in the original town walls there are interval and angle bastions. All the walls of Lo Manthang received a clay rendering and were whitewashed, with the exception of the walls protecting the Choeda which, like the monasteries, were painted red. The central bastion of the eastern wall was also painted red, indicating that it played a religious as well as a defensive role.

The water supply was provided by a stream, fed by the melting mountain glaciers, that runs in a gully alongside the western wall from which channels led to irrigate the neighbouring fields.

The other monasteries of Mustang

Although the population of Mustang has always been small it has managed to support upwards of 15 monasteries of varying sizes. Two are found in the only other towns in Mustang. Kagbeni lies at the confluence of the river Kali Ghandai and one of its tributaries. It was originally protected, in the early Tibetan manner, by its fort. Although the town is not walled the houses are arranged so that the blank outer walls of those on the periphery are contiguous, presenting a defensive appearance to all approaches to the town; three small doorways are the only entrances. Fort and monastery are also found in the walled town of Gemi, south of Lo Manthang. Unlike the capital, however, all the buildings and the town defences are in a poor state of repair.

At Tsarang, midway between these two towns, is an imposing three-storey monastery with a fort-like appearance presenting blank façades externally; the only openings are narrow windows in the top storey. It contains the finest and largest assembly hall in Mustang, however, the monastery is in a poor state of repair. Above the monastery looms a five-storey rectangular fort built on the crest of a ledge that overlooks a deep gorge. The interior is lit by a large central shaft from which radiate many narrow corridors leading to myriad rooms; those containing temples are still in use. Although the fort has many similarities to the palace-fort at Leh it has a much more martial external appearance.

THE DZONGS OF BHUTAN

The Shabdrung and the heavenly abodes of the tantric divinities

Feuding was not limited to the major Buddhist sects. Even within the different factions and individual monasteries rivalries and jealousies could lead to disharmony and occasional violence. In the Drukpa Kakyu monastery of Ralung, to the east of Gyantse, a young monk, Nagawang Namgyal, had been appointed as the 18th abbot. A rival claimant, who had the support of the ruler at Gyantse, challenged this appointment. His high level of intelligence, charisma and ambition were perceived as significant threats to the establishment. His only option was to go into voluntary exile into what is now the western half of the kingdom of Bhutan. He had been invited by the lama of Gasa and was welcomed by many of the inhabitants who had been forced to flee Tibet by the aggressive Gelukpas of Lhasa. It was here that he was to establish his own dynastic lineage amongst these Tibetan Drukpa refugees.

Not subject to Tibetan authority this part of the Himalayas, known in Tibet as 'the southern country of the white rice', was ruled by a loose federation of Drukpa lamas and their supporting minor nobility. Recognized as a devout and reforming lama, Nagawang Namgyal travelled round the valleys gathering disciples and followers as he journeyed. It was now that he acquired the sobriquet 'Shabdrung Rinpoche', literally 'the precious jewel at whose feet one submits'. In a short space of time he had acquired many followers who wished to live under his tutelage either as monks or herdsmen and farmers. As elsewhere in the Tibetan Cultural Region, monastery and fort had a symbiotic relationship. Ever the pragmatist the Shabdrung was to alter this long-standing arrangement. Realizing that his increasing power

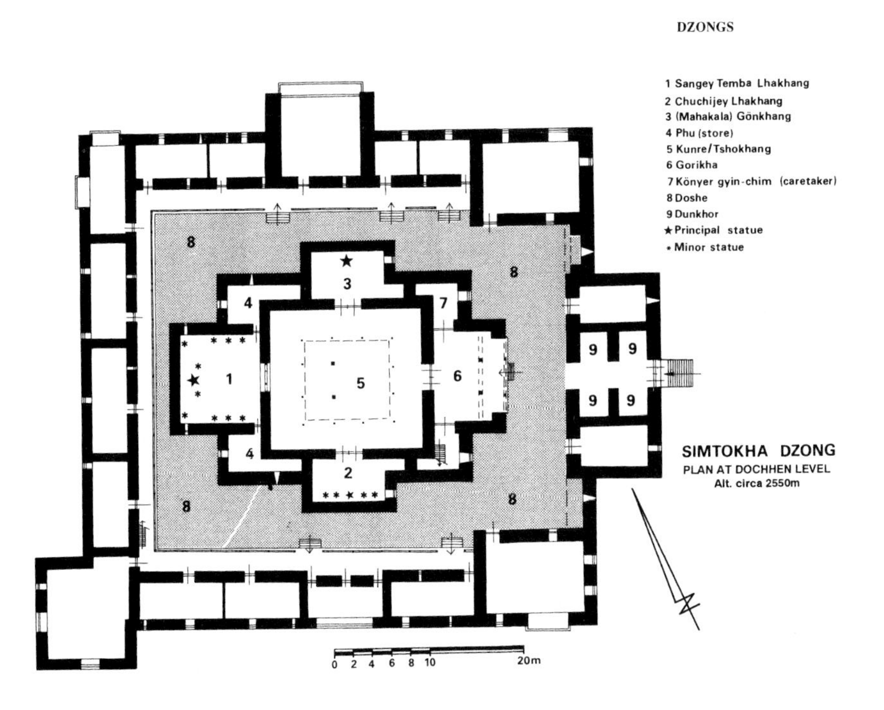

Plan of Simtokha dzong. No. 5 is the *utse*, and 8 the courtyard. (Courtesy of the Minister Ministry of Works and Human Settlement, Royal government of Bhutan)

Simtokha dzong was the first of Ngawang Namgyal's (the Shabdrung) fortress monasteries combining the functions of monastery, administrative centre and fortress. Building commenced in 1629.

and influence was causing concern in central Tibet and consternation amongst certain local lamas, he was to combine the two by building fortress monasteries that were to become unique to Bhutan.

He started building the first of his dzongs in 1629 at Simtokha on the trade route that crossed Bhutan from east to west. It differed both in design and purpose from any other building in the region. Dzongs had existed in the region but were, as in Tibet, forts. He needed a building both to house his monk body and protect them and his lay followers. To do this he created the Bhutanese dzong – a monastery that was a fortress and a fortress that was a monastery. It had to be large enough to accommodate large numbers of his followers and be powerful enough to withstand the military technology of the region. Above all he intended it to be a visible and tangible expression of his power and the permanence of his lineage. Simtokha was to become a rough template for the 16 historical dzongs that are still found in the kingdom.

The dzong of Wangdue Phodrang follows the contours of the spur upon which it was built.

The characteristics of Bhutanese dzongs

Role and function

The architecture is monumental and they are built in traditional Tibetan fashion with inwardly sloping walls and containing windows that increase in size with each storey. The lowest are, in effect, arrow loops or ventilation holes for storerooms. The highest storey contains projecting wooden balconies. Although many have been rebuilt and repaired over the centuries they function today much as they have always done

D SIMTOKHA DZONG, CENTRAL BHUTAN

Although attacked on a number of occasions in the 17th century by Tibetan invaders and their dissident Bhutanese allies, its resolute defenders ensured that the Shabdrung was never defeated. The arms and armour of the officer class contrast markedly with those of the ordinary soldiery. In the middle ground, to the left, are a number of *hsuan feng* (whirlwind) or Chinese trebuchets. They are powered by the muscle power of soldiers heaving, in unison, on a large number of ropes.

with one exception – over the last 150 years or so they have lost their role as places of refuge and as a consequence their military architecture is being gradually lost; a result of rebuilding following earthquake or fire. In addition new dzongs are being built devoid of any form of fortification and the original wooden shingles have been replaced with galvanized tin sheeting.

Over the course of the Shabdrung's lifetime, and for half a century afterwards, a whole series of dzongs were built as the independent state grew and these buildings are found throughout Bhutan. Legend and belief has it that the sites chosen had magical and sacred significance. Military historians will recognize that each dzong is strategically positioned: guarding an invasion route from Tibet to the north or India to the south; to guarding a trade route and acting as a customs post; or serving as a frontier fortress as Bhutan's sphere of influence extended eastwards. They served as barracks and armouries, accommodated the local administrators and served as storehouses for agrarian produce. As the Shabdrung's rule over the country became increasingly secure the dzong developed more of a social role; a place of congregation and celebration, especially for the Tshechus, the masked dance festivals ubiquitous throughout the country.

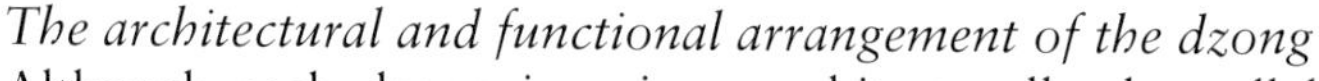

The architectural and functional arrangement of the dzong

Although each dzong is unique architecturally they all had to serve the functions described above. They were designed to a common plan with local variations. In general the external appearances are typically Tibetan. In contrast to the flat roofs found in the arid regions of Tibet, roofs are gently pitched, reflecting the greater rainfall in the Himalayas. Pine rafters carried pine shingle roofs weighed down with heavy stones, resulting in a clear space between the roof and the wall tops. Without exception, immediately below the roof level is a broad band, painted red madder, known as the Khemar that denotes that the building serves a religious function. It contrasts with the light grey clay coloured walls of the dzongs.

The internal arrangement around the stone-flagged courtyard shows the magnificent carpentry of the secular quarters of Jakaryugyel dzong. In the middle distance is the central *utse* with a passageway leading to a replication of the secular quarters but for the exclusive use of the monk body.

Dzongs are either square or rectangular when built on flat ground, although that at Gasa has a rounded front. When built on the crest or a spur of a hill the physical characteristics of the land are usually followed to take advantage of any natural defensive features.

Usually the dzong is divided into two distinct areas – one for the civil and secular administration and the protecting garrison, the other to accommodate the substantial monk body, their teachers and lamas. A central tower or *utse* usually separates the two. This is the most important building in the dzong; it is invariably square or oblong and is multi storeyed. Here are found the main temples of the monastic fortress. In addition it is frequently where the abbot lives and contains the *gonkhang*, the home and 'inner sanctum' of the protective deities. The *utse* also served as a defensive tower and is believed to be a development of the defensive towers of a much earlier age found in Tibet.

The buildings, for both spiritual and temporal needs, are arranged around a stone-flagged courtyard, the *dochen*, on three of its sides. Although there is a clear division functionally between the two there is no architectural difference in the buildings arranged round the *dochens*. Built against the outer dzong walls are two or three tiers of rooms with verandas or arcades facing inward. The pillars and capitals that support the storey above are intricately carved and beautifully painted with varying shades of reds predominating. The interiors of Bhutanese dzongs are incredibly beautiful. Carvings, wall hangings, paintings and statuary decorate most of the rooms, while woodblock books, musical instruments and Buddhist religious images are everywhere. Below these rooms and galleries are found the storerooms for cereals, notably barley and buckwheat, together with butter and dried or cured meat. These foodstuffs were provided by the dependent neighbouring lay population as a form of tax, to safeguard against famine, natural disasters or civil strife. Invariably the *utse* is separated from the courtyards by a pathway required for 'pious clockwise circumambulation'.

The civil quarters required rooms for offices, records, the armoury, stables and accommodation for the administrators (until recent times, monks) and their temporal needs. The monks' quarters provided prayer-halls, classrooms, temples, dormitories, kitchens, a refectory and the monastic library. Each dzong has a main entrance invariably leading to the administrative quarter, usually at first-storey level, reached by retractable wooden ladders carved out of pine trunks. Inside were guardrooms and the huge wooden doors were frequently iron clad. Running all around the dzong under the eaves was, sometimes, a 'chemin de ronde', an unobstructed corridor giving free access for the defenders. Arrow and gun loops enabled an active defence to be offered. In times of perceived danger and potential attack roofs were taken off towers and stone-throwing catapults stored under the eaves reassembled. There is some evidence that some of the towers had cantilevered fighting platforms with mud-brick parapets on their tops.

White's photograph of Paro dzong (1905) illustrates the defensive complex that was to be found at many of the Shabdrung's dzongs. Above the fortress monastery is the *ta* dzong with a fortified bridge in the foreground. The dzong is surrounded by an outer enceinte.

Photographed in 1999 from the *ta* dzong the appearance of the dzong has changed. The dzong burnt down in 1906 and during rebuilding the two *utses*, seen in White's photograph, have been replaced with a solitary central temple keep.

Around a number of dzongs there is evidence of outer defences. This is particularly true at Paro where the Ringpung dzong (the 'fortress of the heap of jewels') is still surrounded on three sides by a wall of varying height. Although neglected and becoming ruinous it is one of the few examples of military architecture that retain evidence of crenellations and is reinforced with square, loopholed towers. These towers, often located at the four corners of the outer enceinte, are known as dzongchungs (literally small dzongs). At

The dzong at Trongsa is the largest and most complex in Bhutan. Viewed from the south the imposing *ta* dzong can be seen at the upper right together with its two outlying towers. The buildings of the town, to the left above the dzong, were built comparatively recently.

E PUNAKHA DZONG, BHUTAN, AS IT MAY HAVE LOOKED AT THE END OF THE 17TH CENTURY

The barbican, in the left foreground, is based on the *ta* dzong that still remains at Trongsa dzong. That at Punakha was washed away in a flash flood. Of the two fortified bridges only one of the blockhouses now survives. The dzong is still at risk from further flooding.

some dzongs, for example at Jakaryugel dzong, the entrance is protected by a fore work that served as a barbican.

Although sieges were a short-term affair, water supplies were ever a problem. There is no written, archaeological or folklore evidence of wells or cisterns, and yet a water supply would be essential. At a number of dzongs that were built above rivers the solution was to build a covered way from the dzong, loopholed and reinforced with a number of round towers, leading down to a water source, either a river or a spring over which was built a round tower known as the chudzong or river tower. The best example is to be found at Jakaryugel dzong.

Dzongs built near to rivers were further protected by cantilevered bridges, built of squared pine logs, defended at each approach by a three- or four-storeyed loopholed tower. Most have been replaced by modern structures but one remains more or less intact at Paro.

The siting of dzongs was always dictated by a high lama 'spurred on by spiritual forces'; whilst they were all strategically placed and natural features incorporated, a number were overlooked by high ground within

ABOVE
Above the solitary entrance to the multistoreyed *ta* dzong at Paro is the red madder band that in Bhutan indicates that the building also serves a religious function.

RIGHT
This view of the *ta* dzong at Trongsa shows how the outlying fort, built at the high point overlooking its dzong, adapts to the sloping ground.

catapult range. This is especially true at Paro and Trongsa. To protect the dzong, outlying forts were built to prevent access to this overlooking high ground. Known as *ta* (or defence) dzongs, the one at Paro is circular, of seven storeys and has walls 2.5m (8ft) thick. Previously used as a prison it is now the home of the National Museum. Internally a removable staircase isolates the top three storeys. Reputably an underground passage is said to run down to the dzong it overlooks.

The *ta* dzong at Trongsa is a complex fortification and dominates the lower-lying dzong built on a mountainside crest. Colloquially known as the 'Tiger's Fortress' it was built to protect the dzong builders. This dzong, constructed on the orders of the Shabdrung as a springboard for his conquest of the eastern part of Bhutan, was started in 1647. It was to become the residence of the kings of Bhutan. On the high ground to the north-east of the dzong the *ta* dzong comprises a five-storey round tower, containing two temples; it is connected from its south-east and south-west aspects to two smaller round towers at a lower level by covered ways that run for about 20m (65ft). Further down the mountainside are two isolated round towers that flank the fort. The *utse* at Trongsa is believed to date from 1543 and is thought to be a derivative of the Khar towers of Tibet.

At some distance from these fortress monasteries were built isolated watchtowers, up and down the valleys, to give early warning of approaching belligerents so that the dzongs were not caught unawares.

AFTERMATH

Destruction, neglect and changing circumstances

The great period of monastery building in the Tibetan Cultural Region started in the 15th century and reached its zenith in the 17th century, paradoxically at a time when the region came under threat from both internal and external forces. The decision by the various kingdoms, principalities and theocracies of the region to maintain their isolation from the world in general and the west in particular ensured that outside architectural influences did not occur, with the exception of Chinese decorative architecture. The dzongs and monasteries that had evolved in the Middle Ages did not undergo any further changes. Nothing much was to change until the end of the 19th century with the exception of those brought about by maintenance, repair and, where required, restoration.

Tibet

The Chinese occupation of Tibet in 1951 has proved disastrous for its Buddhist architectural, artistic, cultural and religious heritage. Such was the Chinese determination to dismantle the feudal theocracy that rebellion broke out in the east of the country where the warrior Khampa attacked Communist cadres and the People's Liberation Army garrisons. By 1957 opposition to the Chinese and their reforming zeal had spread to the whole of the country. Guerrilla warfare was endemic. In retaliation those monasteries and monks who had helped or sheltered the guerrillas were attacked by the PLA using mortars, artillery and, where resistance proved protracted, by bombing. At Litang in eastern Tibet over 3,000 armed monks and farmers occupied the monastery. After a month-long siege with no prospect of capitulation the PLA called in the air force from China and a single Tupolev long-distance heavy bomber pounded the defenders into submission. This was repeated

wherever resistance was met. By 1959 the cause was lost, the Dalai Lama had fled to India and the five-star Red flag flew over the Potala Palace. Many monasteries had suffered severe damage and thousands of monks had fled the country.

In 1966 Tibet got caught up in the Cultural Revolution and in an attempt to destroy Tibetan culture almost every monastery and dzong was reduced to rubble; every building over two storeys that could be used by guerrillas was flattened. In addition much of the religious imagery that had not been spirited away by fleeing monks was looted and transported to China.

A change of heart in the 1980s has seen the gradual rebuilding of a few monasteries by a small number of monks in a manner faithful to the past. What has happened is seen, by monks and lamas, as just an interlude in the cycle of birth, death and rebirth. The political and controlling power of the lamas has gone, probably for ever. The feudal serfdom controlled by the Dalai Lama has been replaced by Chinese Communist directives.

Ladakh and the 'hidden valleys'

The invasion of Ladakh in 1841 by Zowar Singh and his Dogra army resulted in much damage to the monasteries and palaces. In particular the Namgyal palace at Leh was badly damaged and the fortified monastery of Hanle captured and ransacked. The royal family became impoverished and monies were not available for the upkeep of the palaces at Shey, Basgo and Temisgang all of which became neglected, uninhabitable and ruinous. Although Ladakhi independence had been lost, the monasteries fared better. The Dogras recognized the importance of Buddhism to the Ladakhi population and allowed the monasteries to regenerate and to function as they had always

The two round towers to the left of Drukgyel dzong were built to protect the covered way to the underground spring underneath the lowest tower enabling the defenders access to a water supply under cover in times of siege. The covered way and towers are in ruins.

F **THE ATTACK ON LITANG MONASTERY**

In 1956 the people of Litang organized a militia to defend their monastery. When the Chinese killed their leader Yonru-Pon, the Khampa rose in revolt and the Chinese PLA besieged the monastery for over a month. Despite being subjected to artillery and mortar fire the monastery held out. Fearing huge casualties in a frontal assault a single Russian Tupolev TU 4 bomber of the Chinese air force repeatedly bombed the monastery, killing hundreds of monks and militia.

Ruins of the Drukgyel dzong after a fire caused by a butter lamp in 1951.

This photograph of the armoury at Drukgyel dzong was taken by Captain Hyslop of the 93rd Highlanders in 1907. Hyslop wrote: 'Arriving in the inner court we dismounted and were led up ladders to the guest changer or armoury as it appeared for the walls were covered with bows and arrows, leather shields, quaint old guns, and quantities of saddle cloths, wonderful bridles and other horse furniture.' (Courtesy of Beryl Hartley)

done and maintain their links with Lhasa. Their defensive role, however, was over and ongoing repairs and alterations have seen the eroding of defensive architecture.

Ladakh, within its mountainous barriers, remained cut off for most of the year from outside influences until Indian Independence in 1947; the remote valleys of Zanskar, Lahaul and Spiti even more so. Zanskar, for example, did not have access to motorized transport until 1980.

Mustang, Nepal

The area remains remote to this day and until recently had little contact with western ideas, technology and visitors. In addition Nepalese control of the region was minimal. The culture and way of life remained firmly Tibetan and medieval until the 1950s. The invasion of Tibet by the PLA saw an influx of Tibetan refugees, mainly Khampa, a number of whom were trained by the Central Intelligence Agency (CIA) in guerrilla warfare. In turn they formed bands of insurgents who mounted raids into Tibet. As a consequence the PLA needed to deploy large numbers of soldiers to guard the Tibet–Xingiang highway. The CIA also used them as intelligence gatherers and arms were supplied by airdrops. A change in Sino-American relations resulted in the Khampa guerrillas being abandoned by the CIA and all raids into Tibet had ceased by 1970.

Although the area still remains a sensitive one, it is opening up to tourists, especially trekkers. As a consequence funds are becoming available for the repair of the region's medieval buildings and religious iconography.

Bhutan

During the 19th century the various *penlops* vied for power but at the turn of the 20th century Ugyen Wanchuk, the Trongsa *penlop*, ruled and controlled most of central Bhutan. In addition he had become involved with the British as a negotiator. His contribution, at Gyantse in 1904, to talks between the Younghusband mission and the Tibetan hierarchy earned him great respect and with the aid of Britain he was installed as the ruler of the whole of the country on 17 December 1907. His descendants ruled as autocratic kings until very recently.

The dynastic royal family achieved stability and have ensured that the Bhutanese Buddhist traditions have continued; achieved to a large degree by excluding outside influences (it is only in the last decade that its population has had access to television). One major consequence is that its dzongs still function as they have always done with the exception that their fortress role ceased after the 20-year-long civil war which ended in 1885.

LEFT AND NEXT PAGE
These three illustrations show how Punakha dzong has changed. The watercolour by Davis dating from 1783 and the photograph over a century later, by White, show that the dzong has undergone little structural change superficially although after the fire of 1798 new temples were added. The photograph, taken in 1999, of the dzong shows how much the dzong has altered following flood damage and fire in the 20th century. In addition the two fortified bridges have gone and the fore work lost its military role. (The painting by Davis is courtesy of the Yale Centre for British Art)

Since this time dzong architecture has undergone, in many instances, major changes. Physical damage from earthquakes, floods and fires has resulted in major rebuilding. On each occasion more of the martial defensive architecture has been lost. In some instances the original dzong has been demolished and replaced by a modern building, albeit in the traditional Bhutanese style. This is the case in the capital, Thimphu. Here the fortress monastery of Taschicoe has been replaced by a building to house the government and its ministries, the royal family and to serve as a monastery. No vestiges of the fortress role of its predecessor have survived. Fortunately the efforts of two men have enabled the evolution of these fortress monasteries to be recorded and studied.

The drawings and paintings of Samuel Davis and the photographs of John Claude White

Unlike the monasteries of Christendom, the majority of which now lie ruinous and abandoned in Europe, the majority of the monasteries in the region, other than those destroyed by the Chinese in Tibet, are 'living' in the sense that they are still occupied by monks and are continuously undergoing repair and rebuilding using materials, techniques and architectural styles from the past. However, whereas the ruined Christian monasteries are stranded, architecturally, in a time warp this is not the case in the Tibetan Cultural Region. Changes in circumstances and natural and man-made disasters have resulted in an architectural evolution where constructions and buildings no longer required are not replicated.

Although the number of Buddhist fortified and fortress monasteries will never be known, history in the form of paintings, photographs and travelogues illustrate progressive architectural changes. This is particularly true of Bhutan where a significant number of the drawings and paintings of its dzongs by Samuel Davis have survived from his visit in 1783. Whilst a lieutenant in the army of the East Indian Company he had travelled with the mission led by Samuel Turner into Bhutan and Tibet. His role was that of a surveyor and artist. His works are the only visual records we have prior to the 20th century, although they depict the fortress monasteries as they were well over a century after they were first built. In addition his travelogue survives.

A century later, John Claude White began photographing in the Himalayas. As the first British Political Officer based in Gangtok, the capital of Sikkim,

BELOW AND NEXT PAGE
The three illustrations of Tashichoe dzong in Thimphu tell a different story. There is little difference between the watercolour by Davis painted in 1783 and the photograph by White at the turn of the 20th century. The dzong was completely renovated and enlarged by King Jigme Wangchuk between 1962 and 1969. As well as losing its fortress role there are no vestiges of its military architecture remaining. (The painting by Davis is courtesy of the Yale Centre for British Art)

he travelled extensively in the region, especially Bhutan and Tibet where he accompanied the Younghusband Mission. As a very accomplished photographer his portfolio comprises landscapes, portraits and buildings. His photographs of the Bhutanese dzongs show that until the start of the 20th century the Bhutanese dzongs retained their powerful fortress appearances, much as they were when seen by Davis. The photographs in the *Bhutan Times* publication, *The Dzongs of Bhutan*, published in 2000, by comparison show just how many have been remodelled over the last 100 years. As a consequence the volumes of White's photographs are an invaluable record of the unique creations of the Shabdrung.

In addition, together with the invention of the panoramic camera and the photographs of a number of his fellow officers, White's journey, in 1904, to Lhasa is a phenomenal photographic record of buildings now lost, the British Indian Army, the terrain it crossed and the dzongs and monasteries encountered. The fortifications of Tibet have escaped the attentions of architectural historians and White's photographs are the earliest visual records available.

THE SITES TODAY

Tibet

Although the Chinese recognize the importance of revenue obtained from tourism, many areas of the Tibetan Autonomous Region are still out of bounds. The dzong at Gyantse, although badly damaged by the British, has been restored and gives a good insight into the size, power and dominance of these huge forts. It contains a small museum entitled 'the Memorial Hall of the Anti-British'. All the other dzongs throughout the region are little more than piles of rubble.

The Potala Palace was saved from destruction by Zhou Enlai and is still revered by many Tibetans. Its political importance has gone, however, and its religious role has been much diminished. Tourists now greatly outnumber resident monks.

Fortress monasteries of Central Tibet destroyed during the Cultural Revolution

Although all the following monasteries were extensively destroyed by being blown up, almost all have undergone some rebuilding of their Buddhist temples.

Chingwa Taktse, the 'Chingwa Mountain Tiger-Top'. 27km (17 miles) south of Tsetang.

A dzong was built here on the back of a ridge near the fortified palace of the early kings of Tibet. The room in which the Great Fifth was born in 1617 is the principal shrine in the dzong. Although restored in the 18th century it is now ruinous.

Dingpoche, Upper Dranang Valley.

Founded in 1567 during the Civil War it was built on a natural defensive flat-topped spur 300m (1,000ft) above the valley and the monastery was surrounded by defensive walls. It had a dzong as its neighbour in a similar way to Gyantse.

Dratang, 25km (16 miles) east of Samye.

The main temples were enclosed in defensive walls, of which a 750m (2,460ft) stretch survives.

Jampaling, also known as Old Mindoling, 23km (14 miles) east of Samye.

Founded in 1472 the massive and extensive fortified walls enclosed a huge, now totally ruinous, area which once contained nine major temples.

Nalendra, south-west of Langtang.

Founded in 1435 the monastery was one of the principal seats of learning until 1959 when the monastery was totally destroyed by explosives. The fortified walls remain.

Nartang, 18km (11 miles) west of Shigatse.

Once known as the 'Library of Tibet' on account of its sacred book production, the ruins are enclosed by a mud-brick wall approximately 250m square (2,690 square foot).

Ngari Dratsang, south of Tsetang.

Built on an eminence to defend the entrance to the Yon Valley, the Gelukpa fortified monastic college was built in 1541 by the second Dalai Lama to train novices from the far west of Tibet. Looted recently by the Chinese it, paradoxically, once contained treasures plundered by the Tibetan army from Central Asia in the early middle ages.

Gonkar dzong, until its wanton destruction after the Chinese invasion of Tibet in 1951, was the seat of government for the whole of the Gonkar region.

Sakya, the North Monastery.

Although the South Monastery escaped unscathed the North Monastery was almost totally destroyed apart from its fortified enceinte.

Shalu, 20km (12 miles) south of Shigatse.

This fortified monastery, like the South Monastery at Sakya, was rebuilt in the 15th century, protected by inwardly sloping defensive walls in the Mongolian style, after its destruction by an earthquake.

Tingri Shelkar, located near the Nepalese border north of Kathmandu.

Founded in 1266 above the village, the old dzong on the upper slopes of Mount Selkar Dorge contains the ruins of the Yellow Hat monastic complex of Shelkar Chode.

Tsurphu, Pema Kyungdzong, the 'Lotus Eagle Citadel'. 10km (6 miles) north-east of Lhasa.

Founded in the 12th century it became a massive fortress. The walls measure 300m (1,000ft) on each of its four sides and are up to 4m (13ft) thick with powerful corner towers. The monastery contains a 20m (65ft) bronze statue of the Buddha. Built on the high ground on top of the compounds are ruins of a vast 17th-century five-storey residence. The monastery was sacked by the Mongols in 1642 and destroyed in the 1960s by the Chinese to prevent the use of the buildings by Tibetan resistance fighters.

Ladakh

Although entry to Ladakh has become easier over the last few decades the region still remains a sensitive one. The Sino-Indian War and the ongoing dispute between India and Pakistan over Kashmir have ensured that there is a large army presence. This, together with the influx of tourists, has resulted in change to the traditional way of life. This has had a particular effect on monastic recruitment, though some monasteries, such as Hemis and Thiske, are still vibrant and homes to large bodies of monks. Many monasteries welcome visitors; some even provide accommodation. The 'hidden' valleys remain off the tourist routes although trekkers sometimes visit them.

There have been benefits from the opening up of Ladakh. The importance of its architectural heritage has been recognized and the Indian Archaeological Service is restoring Sengge's palace at Leh. In addition the monastic citadel at Basgo, with its huge Maitreya statue and wall paintings, has been restored; how true it is to the original appearance is, however, debatable.

Mustang

This enigmatic backwater remains very isolated from mainstream tourism, although it is visited by trekkers. As a consequence the region is becoming richer, though whether funds will be channelled into the repair of the region's medieval buildings and religious iconography remains to be seen.

The fortress monasteries of Bhutan

All, with the exception of Zhongar and Gasa dzongs, are accessible. They are regarded by the Bhutanese as tangible expressions of their culture, unity and identity, reflecting the religious and political power of the 'dual system'. However, fires and earthquakes have taken their toll over the centuries and with a fortress role no longer required the architecture is changing. Electric lights are replacing butter lamps, and kitchens have become modernized to reduce fire risks. Military architecture is being neglected with rare exceptions.

New dzongs are being built wherein the architecture has evolved to exclude any defensive role.

Daga, the 'fortress of the white auspicious flags of fortune' lies 70km (44 miles) south of Wangdue Phodrang. It was completed in 1651 to protect the southern borders. Built on a ridge it retains its military architecture with a commanding *utse* and barbican.

Dobji, 25km (16 miles) south of Paro this is, perhaps, the oldest surviving dzong and predates the Shabdrung. It was part of a chain of dzongs that protected the trade route from India.

Drukgyel, the 'dzong of the victorious Drukpas' lies 15km (9 miles) north of Paro. Now ruined after a disastrous fire in 1951, it still retains its fortified appearance. Built by the Shabdrung in 1647 to protect the Paro Valley, it was attacked on a number of occasions by the Tibetans. Unusually it contains three courtyards, the first of which served as stables. When visited by White it contained the finest armoury in Bhutan.

Gasa, standing on a hillock in the middle of a pine forest 45km (28 miles) north-west of Paro it was, until a few years ago when ravaged by a disastrous fire, the least altered of the Shabdrung's monastic fortresses. An archaeological survey would probably reveal the outer defences of dzongs, and, possibly, the underground tunnels that allegedly ran between the various fortifications. Its three *ta* dzongs are still intact. Unlike other dzongs the buildings surrounding the central courtyard are arranged in the shape of the letter D.

Haa, built to defend the border with Tibet north of Gasa, is now partially ruinous following a fire in 1913, although its *ta* dzong still stands.

Jakaryugyel, the 'dzong of the White Bird' was built to pacify the Bumthang valleys and is situated on the trans-Bhutan highway. The rebuilt 50m (160ft) Utse is said to be smaller than the original. A barbican protects the solitary entrance and the covered passageway down to the dzong's water supply is still complete with its loopholed parallel walls, reinforcing round towers and *chu* tower.

The covered way running down the hillside at Jakaryugel dzong is the only one left in Bhutan and is in good repair.

Lhuentse, built in 1654 the dzong crowns a crest above the Kuru Chu in eastern Bhutan 70km (44 miles) north of Mongar. There is a rounded entrance tower and the remains of a fortified surrounding wall strengthened with corner towers.

Lingshi, over 100km (60 miles) north of Thimphu the dzong is difficult to reach. Guarding the western border with Tibet it was consecrated between 1667 and 1680. It provided shelter for local shepherds in this sparsely populated region.

Paro, the 'dzong of the Heap of Jewels' was built at the entrance to the Paro Valley. Although the dzong has been rebuilt after a disastrous fire in 1906 many of its ancillary fortifications remain, if somewhat ruinous. Standing on a rock on the eastern bank, the entrance to the monastery was by way of a drawbridge above a dry ditch. Either side of the entrance are guardrooms, where the guards kept mastiffs. Above the dzong is the *ta* dzong (recently restored and now housing the national museum). It is claimed that an underground tunnel runs between the two. Surrounding the monastery is a fortified enceinte reinforced with square towers. The covered way to the chu tower, although much ruined, can still be made out and the *chu* tower remains. A fortified bridge connects the fortress monastery with the opposite bank.

The loopholed covered way terminates at the *chu* or water tower. Steep ladders lead down to the spring that still gushes.

Punakha, 10km (6 miles) north of Wandue Phodrang. The Druk Pungthang Dechen Phodrang, the 'palace of great happiness' stands at the entrance to the Punakha Valley and was the second of the Shabdrung's fortress monasteries. A large fortress, measuring 180 by 70m (590 by 229ft), it was founded in 1637 at the confluence of the Mo and Pho rivers and completed the following year. It has now lost most of its fortifications; the *ta* dzong, which acted as a barbican at the entrance, was seriously damaged in a flash flood in 1960 and has been rebuilt as a temple. The fortified bridges, spanning the two rivers, have been replaced and destroyed. It still acts as the winter quarters of the central monk body and contains the mausoleum temple of the Shabdrung. The tradition of alternating the seat of government and the monk body between here and Taschicoe (Thimphu) started in 1640.

Simtokha, the 'palace of the profound tantric teaching' was built 10km (6 miles) south of the capital, Thimphu. The first of the Shabdrung's dzongs it has been restored a number of times faithful to the original, although the *ta* dzong is now a ruin

Tashichoe, Thimphu. The 'fortress of the auspicious religion' was acquired by the Shabdrung in 1641. After multiple fires the entire dzong has been rebuilt repeatedly; the last time in the 1960s in the traditional fashion. As a consequence all traces of fortification have been lost. Today it houses the government offices and its secretariat. In addition it is the summer residence of the central monk body.

Tashi Yangtse, this dzong was built on the site of a 15th-century dzong. The three-storey *utse* is surrounded by a defensive wall, now much reduced in size. It has been replaced by a newly built dzong nearby. The *ta* and *chu* dzongs are in ruins.

Trashigang, this strategically placed dzong in eastern Bhutan was built in 1659 on the orders of the Trongsa Penlop to spread Drukpa rule and subdue the local petty chieftains. The five-storey *utse* is surrounded by the fortress monastery on a practically impregnable site on the crest of a mountain with steep cliffs on three sides.

Trongsa, built in stages from 1643, is, perhaps, the most impressive of all the dzongs. It consists of a series of buildings, including about 20 temples, all connected by staircases, courtyards and high walls. It was built to control the road running across Bhutan which, at one stage ran through the dzong. From here the Shabdrung embarked on the pacification of eastern Bhutan. Highly visible, it occupies the crest of a ridge that sticks out into a gorge of the Mangu Chu. It is overlooked by the powerful multi-towered *ta* dzong.

Straddling the road running through Bhutan from the east to the west in the centre of the country is Trongsa dzong, once the official residence of the King of Bhutan. The western gateway led to a passage through the dzong to its eastern gate and ensured that all traffic could be monitored and controlled. Fortunately Trongsa dzong has escaped much of the rebuilding that other dzongs have been subjected to.

Wangdue Phodrang, 70km (44 miles) east of Thimphu. Built on a ridge at the confluence of the Punatasang and Dang rivers, this dzong was strategically important as i overlooked routes north–south and east–west. The original dzong of 1638 contains the *utse* and was enlarged in 1683 with the addition of a second building containing a courtyard, the two parts separated by a bridged ravine. A unique cantilevered fortified bridge of two spans crossed the river Punatasang. The central tower contained atemple. Unfortunately floods destroyed the bridge in 1968.

Zhongar, the dzong replaced an earlier castle on the site. Built in the 17th century it burnt down in 1889 and is ruinous as well as inaccessible, and has been replaced by the modern dzong at Mongar.

FURTHER READING

Many of the paintings and sketches of Samuel Davis, together with parts of his journal, are to be found in *Views of Medieval Bhutan*. The Meyers have collected many of John Claude White's photographs taken on his travels and they have been published in *In the Shadow of the Himalayas*. In addition White's papers in the *National Geographic* magazines are illustrated with his photographs.

Aris, M., *Views of Medieval Bhutan* Serinda Publications: London, 1982
Collister, P. *Bhutan and the British* UBS Publishers' Distributors Ltd.: New Delhi, 1987
Francke, A. H., *A History of Western Tibet* Motilal Banarsidass Publishers Pvt. Ltd.: Dehli (Revised Edition), 1998
Gyaltsan, T. (ed.), *The Potala-Holy place in the Snow Land* China Travel and Tourism Press: Beihing, 1994
Heath, I., *Armies of the Nineteenth Century; Asia. 1: Central Asia and the Himalayan Kingdoms* Foundry Books: Guernsey, 1998
Howard, N. F., 'Royal Fortresses of Ladakh', *Archaeology Today* (May 1987), pp. 29–35
Kaul, H. N., *Rediscovery of Ladakh* Indus Publishing Company: New Delhi, 1998
Lhalungpa, Lobsang P., *Tibet: The Sacred Realm* Aperture Inc.: New York, 1983
LaRocca, D. J., *Warriors of the Himalayas* Yale University Press: New Haven, 2006
Meyer, F., 'The Potala Palace of the Dalai Lamas in Lhasa' *Orientations* (July 1987), pp. 14–32
Meyer, K., and Meyer, P. D., *In the Shadow of the Himalayas* Mapin Publishing: India, 2007
Ottley, W. J., *With Mounted Infantry in Tibet* Smith, Elder, & Co.: London, 1906
Peissel, M., *Tibetan Pilgrimage* Abrams: New York, 2005
——, *Mustang, A Lost Tibetan Kingdom* Collins and Harvill Press: London, 1968
——, *Zanskar, The Hidden Kingdom* Collins and Harvill Press: London, 1979
Rajesh, M. N., *The Buddhist Monastery* Lustre Press Pvt. Ltd.: New Delhi, 1998
Rizvi, J., *Ladakh-Crossroads of High Asia* Oxford University Press: New Delhi, 2004
Snellgrove, D., and Richardson, H., *A Cultural History of Tibet* Weidenfeld and Nicolson: London, 1986
Snellgrove, D. L., and Skorupski, T., *Cultural Heritage of Ladakh, Vol 1* Aris and Phillips Ltd: Warminster, 1980
Shakya, Tsering, *The Dragon in the Land of Snows* Penguin: London, 1999
Schicklgruber, C., and Pommaret, F., *Bhutan: Mountain Fortress of the Gods* Bookwise Pvt. Ltd.: India, 1997
Singh, Neetu D. J., and Singh, D. J., *Ladakh* Brijbasi Printers Pvt. Ltd.: New Delhi, 1994
Tenzing, Dorjee, *An Introduction to the Traditional Architecture of Bhutan* Department of Works, Housing and Roads: Thimphu, 1993
——, *The Dzongs of Bhutan: Fortresses of the Dragon Kingdom* Bhutan Times Publication: Thimphu, 2006
White, J. Claude, *Sikhim and Bhutan* Low Price Publications Ltd.: New Delhi, 1999 (Reprinted)
——, Castles in the Air: Experiences and Journeys in Unknown Bhutan *The National Geographic Magazine,* (April 1914), pp. 365–455
——, The World's Strangest Capital *The National Geographic Magazine,* XXIX, (March 1916), pp. 273-295

GLOSSARY

Avalokitesvara 'The Lord who looks down', the compassionate patron divinity of Tibet.

Chorten A stone, brick or mud building containing Buddhist relics and occasionally the cremated remains of senior lamas.

Chu	is Tibetan for a river.
Dalai Lama	The name given to the head of the Gelukpa Buddhist sect by the Mongol leader in 1578. Dalai means Ocean.
Desi	The name given to the temporal ruler of Tibet and Bhutan.
Dochen	is a stone flagged courtyard in a Bhutanese dzong.
Dogras	Inhabitants of the Jammu region of Jammu and Kashmir.
Dzong	Is translated as fortress and this is the meaning in Tibet. In Bhutan it is the name given to the fortress-monastery housing the dual system of secular administrators and the Drukpa monastic monks.
Dzongpon	'The lord of the dzong', was a regional provincial ruler and administrator in Tibet.
Dukhang	The main holy assembly hall of a monastery or Gompa.
Gompa	'A solitary place', the name given to Buddhist monasteries in parts of the western Himalayas.
Gonkhang	The temple housing the guardian deities and sometimes an armoury as at Likir.
Lama	commonly the name given to a Buddhist monk by Westerners. Lama means teacher and refers to a fully ordained and often senior monk.
Maitreya	An image of the future Buddha, usually a statue of huge proportions and found in many temples.
Mongol	A generic name given to an inhabitant of the Mongolian and neighbouring steppes belonging to Mongolic and Turkic tribes united by Genghis Khan.
Pashm	The soft and highly sought after wool that is the winter growth of the pashmina goat used in the manufacture of cashmere shawls.
Ta	is a Tibetan word meaning 'defence'. When linked to dzong it is the name given to an isolated outwork protecting a vulnerable approach to a Bhutanese dzong.
Tantric Tibetan Buddhism	A complex branch of Buddhism based on secret writings of mystical and esoteric significance directing adherents onto the 'path of enlightenment'.
Utse	The central tower of a Bhutanese dzong accommodating the most important temples. It also served as a keep.

INDEX

References to illustrations are shown in bold. Plates are shown with page and caption locators in brackets.